Communications
in Computer and Information Science   606

Commenced Publication in 2007
Founding and Former Series Editors:
Alfredo Cuzzocrea, Dominik Ślęzak, and Xiaokang Yang

Fernando Koch · Andrew Koster
Tiago Primo (Eds.)

Social Computing in Digital Education

First International Workshop, SOCIALEDU 2015
Stanford, CA, USA, August 19, 2015
Revised Selected Papers

 Springer

Editors

Fernando Koch
Samsung Research Institute
Campinas, São Paulo
Brazil

Andrew Koster
Samsung Research Institute
Campinas
Brazil

Tiago Primo
Samsung Research Institute
Campinas, São Paulo
Brazil

ISSN 1865-0929   ISSN 1865-0937   (electronic)
Communications in Computer and Information Science
ISBN 978-3-319-39671-2   ISBN 978-3-319-39672-9   (eBook)
DOI 10.1007/978-3-319-39672-9

Library of Congress Control Number: 2016940006

Printed on acid-free paper

This Springer imprint is published by Springer Nature
The registered company is Springer International Publishing AG Switzerland

Foreword

"Why are students in the 21st century still being taught by 20th-century teachers in 19th-century classroom?"

The media often uses the above quote to criticize poor educational systems and environments. In the meantime the global digital contents market grew more than 20-fold during past 5 years and its projected global market share for 2016 is 36 %. Despite great improvements in various sectors thanks to the progress achieved in digital technologies, I believe that the expression holds true, partly or completely, on a global level.

An advanced education system contributes immensely to the prosperity of a nation. Many global initiatives show that a well-applied digital education system can significantly improve students' performance with low running costs. Digital education with new approaches based on social computing, big data, artificial intelligence, and other emerging technologies will provide students with diverse and new ways of interacting, learning, and exploring the knowledge.

A number of corporations have already initiated important and tangible projects. One project called "Coders of Tomorrow" started by Samsung Research Institute Brazil in 2014 is a system to teach computer programming to children aged 12–15 years from low-income communities and remote areas. The project is part of an even bigger initiative called "Education for Tomorrow," which comprises an introduction to social computation and computational intelligence in order to promote an ideal digital education for all.

In "Education for Tomorrow," the classrooms are equipped with sensors feeding data directly to an intelligent personalization system that interprets the data at near real-time for suitable content recommendation and behavior feedback to each student. Such an environment demands new artificial intelligence and learning analytic techniques to cope with multimodal sensory data, correlate human behavior, learn parameters and resources, and recommend the best course of action.

In order to find new techniques and models to understand the impact of social behavior on learning, and the learning context upon learning performance, we organized the First International Workshop on Social Computing in Digital Education, held at Stanford University, in August 2015. The workshop focused mainly on the following issues:

– Novel data mining and machine learning for social intelligence in digital education
– Social modelling and simulation to investigate social behaviors, emotional intelligence, processes, and other social aspects that may influence learning performance in an educational environment
– Smart education platform and interactive systems of social computing in digital education
– Analysis of social media and media intelligence in digital education

- Mobile social gaming in digital education
- Utilization of mobile and wearable technology in social systems in digital education, among others

This book contains nine papers selected from the proceedings by the members of the Program Committee. The papers represent a broad range of cutting-edge areas in social computing and artificial intelligence such as content selection and recommendation, gamification, machine learning, knowledge management, learning environment, and smart interaction.

I hope that this book will be stimulating and useful for all those concerned with bringing interactive social intelligence for teaching and learning in the classroom. It is high time for digital education!

April 2016   Yeun Bae Kim

Preface

This volume includes extended and revised versions of a set of selected works from the First International Workshop on Social Computing in Digital Education (SOCIA-LEDU), complemented by some chapters by invited researchers in this field of research. The workshop was hosted in conjunction with the ASE 8th International Conference on Social Computing (SOCIALCOM) on August 19, 2015, at Stanford University, USA.

The purpose of the SOCIALEDU workshops is to bring together researchers and practitioners in the field, and promote discussions around the state-of-the-art research and application of social computing for technology-enhanced learning. The workshop received contributions ranging from top–down experimental approaches and a bottom–up evolution of formal models and computational methods. The research and development discussed is a basis of innovative technologies that allow for intelligent applications, collaborative services, and methods to better understand the role social computing can play in education.

The workshops promoted international discussion forums with submissions from different regions and Program Committee members from many countries in Europe (the Netherlands, Portugal, Spain, Sweden, Germany), Asia and Oceania (Japan, Korea, New Zealand), and the Americas (Brazil, Colombia, USA).

The SOCIALEDU workshop received 10 submissions through the workshop website, from which we selected four full and three short presentations. Six of these papers were selected for publication as extended versions in this volume, together with three invited works. All the papers were reviewed by at least three different reviewers, and the works selected for this volume are representative of research projects around the aforementioned methods. The selections highlight the innovation and contribution to the state of the art, suggesting solutions to real-world problems and applications built upon the proposed technology.

In the first chapter, "Selection of Collaborative Learning Techniques Using Bloom's Taxonomy", Gómez and Moreno propose a recommender system for choosing the right technique in a collaborative learning scenario by matching the competencies required (as described using Bloom's taxonomy) with the competencies that the collaborative learning activity is designed to develop. The work categorizes 26 different collaborative learning activities, and the design and testing of a recommender system for these activities. While collaborative learning has long been recognized as enhancing learning, it is not easy to incorporate such social activities into a regular classroom. Such a recommender system can help identify when a collaborative activity is useful, and what activity can be used; a conclusion they corroborate in their results.

The second chapter, "Gamification of Collaborative Learning Scenarios: Structuring Persuasive Strategies Using Game Elements and Ontologies," by Challco et al., introduces a structured systematization for representing concepts from gamification as used in collaborative learning, and a reasoning method for suggesting ways to gamify collaborative learning scenarios. In particular they focus on gamification as a persuasive technology, and describe an ontological model to structure and organize persuasive strategies, allowing a system to match a user's personality type to specific techniques that can better engage him or her in a collaborative learning scenario.

In the third chapter, "A Full-Body Interaction Game for Children with Hearing Disabilities to Gain the Immersive Experience in a Puppet Show," Egusa et al. describe a novel physical-computational system in which children participate in an interactive puppet show. This puppet show was designed specifically to increase the appreciation of children with hearing disabilities by converting sounds into visual information, and allowing the children to participate through physical, rather than verbal, feedback. The authors present empirical evidence that the system is effective. Such work illustrates how computational techniques can adapt age-old teaching (and play) methods to be inclusive of people with disabilities, traditionally sidelined by such methods.

The fourth chapter, "A Learning Object Recommendation Model with User Mood Characteristics," by Pérez et al., presents a recommender system for learning objects that takes the user's emotions into account when making the recommendation. The technique combines a traditional test of learning style with a system for recognizing emotions, and uses the combination in a collaborative recommendation system to the best learning object for a specific subject.

The fifth chapter, "A Quantitative Analysis of Learning Objects and Their Metadata in Web Repositories," by Carvalho et al., presents a systematic review of the metadata available in different learning object repositories. They find that the organization and structuring of both learning objects and the metadata in online repositories is lacking and there is a lot of work to be done in order to use such repositories for computational reasoning. Despite various different standards for storing metadata, most learning objects are stored without even the most rudimentary metadata tags completed (often there is only a title to accompany a learning object). This systematic quantitative review is valuable for any work intending to use such metadata to select, search, or recommend learning objects automatically.

One such approach for selecting learning objects is described by de Amorim Junior and Silveira in the sixth chapter, titled "Towards an Intelligent Learning Objects-Based Model for Dynamic E-Learning Content Selection." They present an agent-based approach to allow for the adaptability and re-use of learning objects in distance learning applications. Building upon the SCORM API for learning objects and previous work on intelligent learning objects, the authors propose a multi-agent system that can adapt in real-time to student interactions with learning objects and provide alternative or supplementary material. This work incorporates techniques from intelligent tutoring systems, Semantic Web technologies, and multi-agent systems to provide a better way for searching and selecting learning objects.

In the seventh chapter, "The Socio-Cultural Approach to Software Engineering and Its Application to Modelling a Virtual Learning Environment," Gluz et al. present a novel methodology for software engineering, particularly designed for social applications. In this work they apply it in a case study for designing an educational application that selects and adapts learning objects based on ontological information about the learning objects, the student, the teacher's pedagogical strategy, and other information available in the virtual learning environment.

The eighth chapter, "New Moodle Blocks for Knowledge Management," by Sprock and Vicari, proposes and evaluates novel plugins to allow for better knowledge management in the Moodle LMS system. In particular, they designed Yellow Pages, FAQ, and Lessons Learned modules, as well as a tool for monitoring students' activities in Moodle, thereby making Moodle into a more collaborative tool for students as well as teachers.

Finally, the chapter "Experimental Evaluation on Machine Learning Techniques for Human Activities Recognition in Digital Education Context," by Leitão et al., discusses how human activity recognition could be used in a classroom setting to enhance learning analytics, and evaluates a number of different algorithms to distinguish three basic physical activities in a classroom – e.g., sitting, walking, standing – using a cellphone. They find that the PART algorithm achieves good accuracy, and can be embedded in an application for use directly in a cellphone.

We would like to thank all the volunteers who made the workshops possible by helping to organize and peer review the submissions, and to EasyChair for the conference and proceedings management system.

March 2016   Andrew Koster
                                                                             Fernando Koch
                                                                             Tiago Primo

Organization

Program Committee

Ricardo Azambuja Silveira	UFSC, Brazil
Raimundo Barreto	UFAM, Brazil
Maria Rosangela Bez	UFRGS, Brazil
Marta Rosecler Bez	UFRGS, Brazil
Ig Ibert Bittencourt	UFAL, Brazil
Sergio Borger	IBM Research, Brazil
Daniel Cabrera Paniagua	Universidad de Valparaiso, Chile
Carlos Cardonha	IBM Research, Brazil
Andre Carvalho	UFAM, Brazil
Alberto Castro	UFAM, Brazil
Helder Coelho	FCUL, Portugal
Juan Colonna	UFAM, Brazil
Frank Dignum	Universiteit Utrecht, The Netherlands
Néstor Méndez	UNC, Colombia
Christian Guttmann	IVBAR, Sweden
Julian Moreno	UNC, Colombia
Eduardo Oliveira	PUC-PE, Brazil
Hugo Paredes	INESC, Portugal
Alexandre Ribeiro	UCS, Brazil
Jordi Sabater Mir	IIIA-CSIC, Spain
Elder Santos	UFSC, Brazil
Joao Luis Silva	UCS, Brazil
Takao Terano	Tokyo Institute of Technology, Japan
Rosa Vicari	UFRGS, Brazil
Leandro Krug Wives	UFRGS, Brazil

Contents

Selection of Collaborative Learning Techniques Using Bloom's Taxonomy

Sebastián Gómez Jaramillo[1,2(✉)] and Julián Moreno Cadavid[2]

[1] Tecnológico de Antioquia, Medellín, Colombia
sgomezja@tdea.edu.co, sgomezj@unal.edu.co
[2] Universidad Nacional de Colombia, Medellín, Colombia
jmorenol@unal.edu.co

Abstract. This work presents a model for the selection of Collaborative Learning (CL) techniques considering specific characteristics and needs of the activity that teachers want to perform within their educational practice. This model considers the representation of the activity in terms of the required competencies defined from Bloom's taxonomy. Then, using the characterization of a set of techniques conducted by experts, an algorithm is used for providing an affinity measure, doing a recommendation of the technique to use. A validation of the model from three case studies is also described, carried out by comparing experimental and control groups. The results show that CL allows for achieving better academic performance, but also that those techniques proposed by the recommendation model exhibited higher performance.

Keywords: Algorithm · Group learning · Taxonomy · Recommendation · Model

1 Introduction

An important element of teaching is to develop in students useful capabilities for comprehensive training through implementation of various teaching models and learning strategies [1]. In recent decades, the classic teaching method has changed. Teacher is no longer considered the owner of the knowledge and the only one responsible for teaching. The actual teaching methods are interactive and the students are the protagonists of their learning process. As UNESCO mentions [2], there is not a unique and consolidated knowledge, transmitted from teachers, owners of learning and teaching process to students as passive receptors. It is now a community of people seeking, selecting, constructing and communicating collaboratively knowledge, a type of experience that connects directly with the concept of learning communities.

One of these methods, known as Collaborative Learning (CL), where a group of students construct knowledge collaboratively through activities carried out in teams. Each member have an individual responsibility and his interaction with the rest helps to maximizing individual and group learning [3–5]. Collaborative skills are considered one of the essential skills of the XXI century but, in order to reach it, is not enough working in a team, it is also necessary to have effective collaboration inside it [6].

© Springer International Publishing Switzerland 2016
F. Koch et al. (Eds.): SOCIALEDU 2015, CCIS 606, pp. 1–11, 2016.
DOI: 10.1007/978-3-319-39672-9_1

There have been studies to indicate when the interaction within a team generates a good or bad collaboration [7]. Such studies identified that an adequate design on the structuring of teams, the activity to develop and goals to achieve, allows greater collaboration effectiveness [8]. It is recommended to use CL techniques to identify a suitable design for the implementation of CL. Such techniques are characterized for being well structured and to take advantage of social and affective processes generated by the interaction of the students, the division of tasks and roles that each member have in their team [9]. This is supported on the theory that the collaborative cognitive abilities reached after a structured work, have greater scope to just the sum of the individual abilities of each team member [10].

However, selecting a CL technique for a particular educational activity is not easy, particulartly due to the number and diversity of them. Precisely, the contribution of this work is a model for the selection process, which must not be mistaken with the description or comparison of CL techniques. The latter has already been done in numerous researches. For example, Domingo et al. [11] list 41 different techniques and emphasize some, but not suggest a method for selecting one or another. Kagan [12] lists techniques of his own, but not presents a method for selecting them. Walters [13] does make a differentiation of techniques according to their degree of structuring, rewards and level of collaboration, but focuses only in four of them: jigsaw, student team learning, learning together, and group research. Amante & Romero [14] grouped techniques according to their degree of use and type of activity that would be applied: theoretical, practical or mixed. In addition, Alfageme [15] lists and describes some techniques, characterizing them as the purpose, mode of development and own elements. Finally, one of the most complete work is from Barkley, Cross and Howell [16] where deepened over 30 different techniques, describing clearly how you can use. Techniques are divided into categories: for dialogue, for reciprocal teaching, for problem solving, using graphic organizers of information and techniques focused on writing.

2 Bloom'S Taxonomy and Academic Competencies

The aim of the model proposed is to provide a recommendation on which of these more suitable techniques to use in a specific educational activity. To achieve this, the model consists of three elements: a characterization of CL techniques, a characterization of the educational activity, and a mathematical model to map both.

The characterization criteria for educational activities are based on the competences involved. Therefore it is important to define what is meant by competence. Fingel [17] defines it as a combination of knowledge, skills and attitudes appropriate to the context. Meanwhile, Alonso [18] argues that competencies are not a list of contents or concepts or isolated processes, but it is the integration of basic knowledge, general processes and contexts, seeking always to be transversal to different areas of knowledge and also allows students to develop their training.

Both definitions are very general, which is why the proposed model chose to use a more specific characterization using the Bloom's taxonomy [19]. The original idea of this taxonomy is to generate a hierarchy of competencies, with increasing complexity, indicating the level that students can achieve on a given domain. Later, Anderson and

Table 1. Bloom taxonomy revised by Krathwohl and Anderson

Level	Cognitive domain	Cognitive processes
1	Remember	Recognize, remember, list, describe, recover, identify, locate, matching
2	Understand	Interpret, exemplify, classify, compare, summarize, defend, explaining, paraphrase
3	Apply	Execute, implement, solve, use, modify, update
4	Analyze	Differentiate, organize, assign, compare, relate, deconstruct, structuring, integrating
5	Evaluate	Check, criticize, review, organize and conduct hypothesis, experiment, judge, argue
6	Create	Generate, plan, design, construct, devise, draw, invent, mix

Krathwohl [20] proposed a change in the taxonomy, adding a new dimension called cognitive process, based on the verb or action to be achieved. In this dimension, processes are defined by verbs and are organized in hierarchical order, from simple to complex and from concrete to abstract. Each level is divided into cognitive domains and each domain has in turn several possible cognitive processes. They also changed the name of some domains, as well as the order of the last two. Each level goes upward, so for example, if a student is able to evaluate, in theory should have gone through the four previous levels. In Table 1, the whole revised taxonomy is presented.

3 Model Proposed

3.1 Characterization of Educational Activity

The model proposed uses the taxonomy described in previous section to specify the educational goals to be achieved in a given activity. This is because the verbs used in this taxonomy are transversal and can be used to define almost any competence in different domains of knowledge. The description of a competence consists of two parts, the first define the process that seek to achieve, while the second is related to the specific knowledge domain relative to the activity. An example for the domain knowledge "Basic Macroeconomics", considering the first level of taxonomy (Remember) and the process "to describe", would be something like: "The student will be able to describe the law of supply and demand". Meanwhile, an example for the domain knowledge "Reading Comprehension", considering the fourth level (Analyze) and the process "to compare", would be something like: "The student will compare conceptual and formal aspects in each of the texts he/she reads".

3.2 Characterization of CL Techniques

The main aspect in characterization of CL techniques is the description of each technique in terms of Bloom's taxonomy. That is, in terms of cognitive processes involved

Table 2. Preselected CL techniques

1	Think, forms a couple and comment	10	Role playing game	19	Group table
2	Ideas wheel	11	Jigsaw	20	Team matrix
3	Talk groups	12	Testing teams	21	Sequenced chains
4	Pay to talk	13	Troubleshooting by couples thinking aloud	22	Words networks
5	Interview in three steps	14	Pass the problem	23	Diary for dialogue
6	Critical debate	15	Case studies	24	Dyadic essay
7	Taking notes in pairs	16	Structured problem solving	25	Collaborative writing
8	Learning cells	17	Analysis team	26	Team Anthologies
9	Team games tournament	18	Grouping by affinity		

Table 3. Characterization of Jigsaw technique according to experts

Level	Domain	Process		
		High	Medium	Low
1	Remember	Describe	Remember	Identify
2	Understand	Explaining	Exemplify	Summarize
3	Apply			
4	Analyze	Structuring	Organize	Compare
5	Evaluate	Argue	Review	Judge
6	Create			

in each technique. In Table 2, 26 well documented techniques are shortlisted (based on [16]). For their characterization a panel of three experts in CL was involved. They determine if a technique was involved at each level and cognitive process, indicating to what extent did, using a discrete numerical rating from 0 to 5, with 5 being the highest and 0 the lowest score. After repeating the procedure for all the techniques, all ratings were averaged arithmetically level to level, and process by process. For each level the three processes with higher scores were selected. The process with the highest average rating will be assigned a value of 3 (high), the second of 2 (medium) and the third of 1 (low). If a tie occurs between different processes, the technique with more points above zero is selected.

As an example, the technique "Jigsaw" is presented in Table 3 according to score obtained and the order of levels and processes presented in Table 1.

This table is then translated to a numerical matrix with six rows, one for each level, and eight columns, one for each process. Each cell is filled with a numerical value between 0 and 4 for each of the processes presented, in the corresponding order, in Table 2. A value of 3 is assigned to processes with high rating, 2 with medium, 1 with

Table 4. Requirement matrix example

Level	Process							
1	0	2	0	3	0	1	0	0
2	0	2	0	0	1	0	3	0
3	0	0	0	0	0	0	0	0
4	0	2	0	1	0	0	3	0
5	0	0	2	0	0	0	1	3
6	0	0	0	0	0	0	0	0

low, and 0 to those which were not considered. Table 4 shows the translation of the information provided in Table 3 to the corresponding technique matrix (T).

3.3 Selection Process

The purpose of the proposed model is to obtain an intersection between the educational activity that a teacher want to perform and the CL techniques characterized, with Bloom's taxonomy at the common point. For the characterization of the techniques, the model has 26 tables and 26 corresponding matrix, one for each of the selected techniques, with the format presented in Tables 3 and 4 respectively. In the educational activities, it is necessary to quantify the description that teacher made, considering for this purpose only those processes that refer to the corresponding educational goal.

Returning to the first example presented in Sect. 3.1: "The student will be able to describe the law of supply and demand", together with three other processes that may occur in the educational academic activity at various levels of the taxonomy, the resulting characterization is shown in Table 5.

Table 5. Example of an educational activity characterization

Level	High	Medium	Low
1	Describe		
2	Explain	Compare	
3	Use		

As shown in Table 5, for each level up to three processes are chosen with a relative weight between high, medium and low. These data are then translated into a matrix of 6×8 called requirements matrix (R) where rows indicate the levels of the taxonomy and columns indicate each of the processes in the order presented in Table 2. Of the six levels, only level three includes six processes, the others include eight.

Each cell is filled with a numerical value between 0 and 30 for each of the processes described. 30 is assigned to processes with high rating, 20 with medium, 10 with low, and 0 to those which were not considered. Subsequently, from the last level selected (in the example above Level 4), all the cells are filled with a value of -1. This value allows priorizing techniques that are designed to consider to the maximum level selected by

Table 6. Requirement matrix example

Level	Process							
1	0	0	0	30	0	0	0	0
2	0	0	0	20	0	0	30	0
3	0	0	0	30	0	0		
4	−1	−1	−1	−1	−1	−1	−1	−1
5	−1	−1	−1	−1	−1	−1	−1	−1
6	−1	−1	−1	−1	−1	−1	−1	−1

the teacher, subtracting points to the potentially more complex techniques. Table 6 shows the translation of the information provided in Table 5.

Once the requirements matrix R is completed, and considering the techniques matrixes T_k ($1 \leq T_k \leq 26$), model proceeds as follows:

$$A_i^k = \sum_{j=1}^{8} R_{i,j} * T_{i,j} \tag{1}$$

That is, the rows of the requirements matrix are multiplied by rows of techniques matrices to generate a scalar for each level of each technique value.

Vectors are multiplied by the weight vector levels $P = \{10, 12, 14.4, 17.28, 20.73, 24.88\}$. That is:

$$B^k = A_i^k * P \tag{2}$$

The weight vector gives greater priority to the coincidence of processes from higher levels of the taxonomy considering that achieve a certain level process involves the mastery of all or most of the processes of the lower levels. A simple increasing function was used, of type $P_i = \alpha P_{i-1}$ choosing empirically an initial value $P = 10$ and a value for the percentage increase between levels $\alpha = 20 \%$.

To break ties between the B values of different techniques, a value C is calculated:

$$C^k = B^k * (r/s) \tag{3}$$

Where r is the number of common processes between technique k and the requirements matrix, while s is the total amount of process of the requirements matrix.

Finally, in order to present more interpretable results, such a value C is compared to the one of an ideal technique, that is, one that would have an exact match with the processes and priorities defined in the requirements matrix. This value is called C^ϕ, which is calculated as:

$$D^k = \min\left\{\frac{C^k}{C^\phi}, 0\right\} * 100 \tag{4}$$

The higher D^k, considering the range [0, 100], the best suited that technique k is for the educational activity described by the teacher.

4   Validation Methodology

To demonstrate the validity of the presented model three case studies were conducted in real educational environments. In order to do so the teachers involved received training on CL and Bloom's taxonomy. These teachers the defined the educational activity they wanted to accomplish and described it by the model in order to get the requirements matrix.

In each case students were divided into three groups. With the first group the CL technique that obtained the highest score according to the model was used. The second group used the second highest score technique and the last group did not used a technique at all, that is, they worked in groups but in an unstructured way. All students received the same study material and should accomplish the same assessment.

The results analysis was done both quantitatively and qualitatively. The first through the results of the assessment measured on a numerical scale in the range [0, 5] with one decimal place. The second by a perception survey made to participating students, which should be answered by a Likert scale of five values: 1 = strongly disagree, 2 = disagree, 3 = neutral, 4 = agree, 5 = Strongly Agree. This survey was focused on opinion regarding the positive interdependence, one of the principles of CL: "The learning technique employed allowed the participation of my partners improve my individual learning?"

5   Results and Discussion

The first case study was applied in the technology program "Production of footwear and leather" offered by SENA (National Learning Service) in Colombia, within the course "Process Management". The course was made up of 18 students, 10 women and 8 men. Under teacher requirements, the groups should be formed by two students, that is, he had a total of nine teams. Table 7 present the requirements matrix resulting from the characterization made by the teacher to the activity called "Process Outsourcing".

From this matrix and by applying the procedure defined by the model, the "testing teams" technique was obtained first with a score of 38.0 %, followed by "critical debate" technique with a score of 33.7 %. Summarizing, the first technique consists in presenting a study material for each team, then doing an individual test and later corrections are made in team and do again the test as a group. The second technique consists in generating discussion among students promoting the defense of a particular point of view. Three of the six students took the role of being in favor of outsourcing and three students the role of being against. Students had a previous phase where they prepared their arguments and then worked with his partner reaching common ground in the debate.

The second case study was applied in the technology program "Logistics management" offered also by SENA, within the course "Distribution Plant". The course was made up of 18 students, 4 women and 14 men. Under teacher requirements, the groups should have three students, that is, he had a total of six teams. Table 8 present the requirements matrix resulting from the characterization made by the teacher to the activity called "Kinds of stores".

Table 7. Requirement matrix - Case 1

Level	High	Medium	Low
1	Remember	Identify	
2	Interpret	Compare	Explaining
4	Differentiate	Compare	
5	Argue		

Table 8. Requirement matrix - Case 2

Level	High	Medium	Low
1	Identify	Remember	
2	Summarize	Exemplify	Classify
4	Compare	Differentiate	

From this matrix, the "words networks" technique was selected first with a score of 31.63 %, followed by "role playing game" technique with a score of 23.6 %. The first technique consists in assigning students a central theme and, from it, they should generate brainstorm to finally develop a conceptual map from the connection of the ideas generated. The second technique consists in giving each student a role that should be studied and interpreted, one student plays the role of moderator and is responsible for guiding the activity.

Finally, the third case study was implemented in the course "Engineering Seminar II", which is a course for various engineering programs at the National University of Colombia. This was the largest of the three cases composed of 90 students, 62 men and 28 women. Under teacher requirements, the groups should have between four and six students. The formation of the groups was heterogeneously, including students from different programs within each and at least one woman per team. Table 9 present the requirements matrix resulting from the characterization made by the teacher to the activity called "Study of the socio-economic impact".

From this matrix, the "analysis team" technique was selected first with a score of 49.9 %, followed closely by "jigsaw" technique with a score of 47.45 %. The first technique consists in delegating a specialized task that requires a complex analysis of each student, later meeting in team in order to produce a single final report. The second technique consists of three stages. In the first stage a specific topic is assigned to each team member. In the second stage each student prepares a summary of its subject and explains each partner so that all have the same common knowledge. In the third stage they solve a particular problem, which in this case was the preparation of a report.

The results of the quantitative assessment for the three case studies are presented in Table 10. In the case study 1, the technique with second best score obtained a better result than the first, but the difference is less than 1 %, while the first had a lower standard deviation. Meanwhile, groups that did not use technique were had lower results, about 10 % less on average, as well as a higher standard deviation.

In the second case study the differences are larger. The teams that worked with the first technique selected obtained average results 33 % higher than in the second and 75 % over those who did not use any.

In the case study 3, the situation was similar to the first case. The difference in results between the two techniques with the highest score was less than 1 %. Similarly, groups that did not use the technique were the worst performers, about 15 % less on average, and a higher standard deviation.

Finally, the results of the qualitative assessment for the three cases are presented in Table 11. Unlike quantitative results, this did not have such a clear trend. While in all three cases the perception of students when used some of the CL techniques was more positive, or at least equaled, to when they did not, there was not a marked superiority between the first and the second technique selected by the model.

Table 9. Requirement matrix - Case 3

Level	High	Medium	Low
2	Interpret		
4	Structure	organize	Differentiate
5	Argue		

Table 10. Summary of quantitative results of the case studies

Case	Technique	Groups	Tests average	Standard deviation
1	Testing teams	3	4.467	0.058
	Critical debates	3	4.500	0.458
	No technique	3	4.033	0.551
2	Words networks	2	5.000	0.000
	Role playing game	2	3.350	1.202
	No technique	2	1.250	0.636
3	Analysis team	6	4.550	0.432
	Jigsaw	6	4.517	0.382
	No technique	5	3.880	0.512

Table 11. Summary of qualitative results of the case studies

Case	Technique	Average	Standard deviation
1	Testing teams	4.167	0.408
	Critical debates	4.500	0.548
	No technique	4.167	0.753
2	Words networks	4.833	0.408
	Role playing game	4.500	0.548
	No technique	4.167	0.753
3	Analysis team	3.741	1.059
	Jigsaw	3.821	0.863
	No technique	3.636	0.658

6 Conclusions

From the results obtained in carrying out the experimental validation of the model proposed in this article at least four conclusions were identified. First off, both quantitative and qualitative validation shows that the use of this CL in classroom activities turns out to be a good strategy despite of the specific technique used. This can be explained because good structuring of CL techniques promotes positive interdependence.

Second, quantitative results obtained in experimental groups appear to be consistent with the score given by the technique selected by the model in each case. Differences in performance were small in case studies 1 and 3 where the differences of selection scores were not big either. Meanwhile in case 2, where the difference in selection scores was more pronounced, similarly occurred in performance score.

A third finding is that it seems that the score obtained by the technique employed is a good predictor of the performance achieved by students. According to data obtained those techniques with scores above 30 % according to the model demonstrated scores above to 4.5 in a [0,5] scale, indicating that they are on or above 90 %. This however cannot be taken lightly because, unlike the case of test 3, the amount of test subjects on both cases was quite low.

Indeed, one of the future works expected to be realized, corresponding to the fourth finding, is that it is necessary to provide continuity ensuring validations in bigger courses that allow a stronger statistical significance. Besides, it is necessary to calibrate the model variables, particularly those that are involved with matrix techniques, looking for it a greater number of experts to conduct their appreciation from Bloom's taxonomy.

Acknowledgment. The research presented in this article was partially funded by Colciencias program for young researchers and innovators "Virginia Gutiérrez de Pineda" - Generación Bicentenario.

References

1. Núñez del Rio, M.C., Biencito López, C., Carpintero Molina, E., García García, M.: Enfoques de atención a la diversidad, estrategias de aprendizaje y motivación en educación secundaria. Perfiles Educativos **36**(145), 65–80 (2014). Instituto de Investigaciones sobre la Universidad y la Educación, Mexico
2. UNESCO.: Enfoques Estratégicos Sobre Las TICs en Educación en América Latina y el Caribe. Oficina Regional de Educación para América Latina y el Caribe, Santiago de Chile (2013)
3. Dillenbourg, P.: What do you mean by 'collaborative learning'? In: Dillenbourg, P. (ed.) Collaborative-Learning: Cognitive and Computational Approaches, vol. 1, pp. 1–15. Pergamon, Amsterdam (1999)
4. Johnson, D.W., Johnson, R.T., Smith, K.: The state of cooperative learning in postsecondary and professional settings. Educ. Psychol. Rev. **19**, 15–29 (2007). Springer, US

5. Stahl, G., Koschmann, T., Suthers, D.: Computer-supported collaborative learning: An historical perspective. In: Sawyer, K.R. (ed.) Cambridge Handbook of the Learning Sciences, pp. 409–426. Cambridge University Press, Cambridge (2006)
6. Szewkis, E., Nussbaum, M., Rosen, T., Abalos, J., Denardin, F., Caballero, D., Tagle, A., Alcoholado, C.: Collaboration within large groups in the classroom. Int. J. Comput. Support. Collab. Learn. **6**, 561–575 (2011). Springer, US
7. Kwon, K., Liu, Y.H., Johnson, L.P.: Group regulation and social-emotional interactions observed in computer supported collaborative learning: Comparison between good vs. poor collaborators. Comput. Educ. **78**, 185–200 (2014). Elsevier
8. Isotani, S., Mizoguchi, R., Inaba, A., Ikeda, M.: The foundations of a theory-aware authoring tool for CSCL design. Comput. Educ. **54**(4), 809–834 (2010). Elsevier
9. Ruengtam, P.: Modeling of cooperative/ collaborative learning technique : a case study of interior architectural program. Procedia Soc. Behav. Sci. **105**, 360–369 (2013). Elsevier
10. Theiner, G., Allen, C., Goldstone, R.L.: Recognizing group cognition. Cogn. Syst. Res. **11**(4), 378–395 (2010). Elsevier
11. Domingo, J., Llumà, J., Manzanares, M., Ruiz, C., Camps, G.: Estrategias Para el Trabajo con Grupos Colaborativos. In: XII Congreso Universitario de Innovación Educacitva en las Enseñanzas Técnicas, Escuela Universitaria de Ingeniería Técnica Industrial de Barcelona (EUETIB), Barcelona (2004)
12. Kagan, S.: Cooperative Learning. Kagan Editorial, Virginia (1994)
13. Walters, L.: Four Leading Models of Cooperative Learning. Harvard Education Letter Research Online, Masachusets (2000)
14. Amante García, B., Romero García, C.: Estudio comparativo de la introducción de aprendizaje cooperativo en diferentes titulaciones técnicas. Revista Iberoamericana de Educación **42**(2), 1–15 (2007). Organización de Estados Iberoamericanos, Madrid
15. Alfageme González, B.: Modelo colaborativo de enseñanza-aprendizaje en situaciones no presenciales. Un estudio de caso. Universidad de Murcia. Departamento de Didáctica y Organización Escolar, Murcia (2008)
16. Barkley, E., Cross, P., Major, C.: Collaborative Learning Techniques. Jossey-Bass -Wiley, San Francisco (2004)
17. Figel, J.: Competencias clave para el aprendizaje permanente. In: Al tablero, vol. 52. MinEducación, Bogotá (2009)
18. Alonso, R.F.: Educativas : Hacia Un Aprendizaje Genuino. Universidad Complutense de Madrid, Madrid (2008)
19. Bloom, B.S.: Taxonomy of Educational Objectives. David McKay, New York (1956)
20. Krathwohl, D.R.: A Revision of Bloom's Taxonomy : An Oberview. Theory Pract. **41**(4), 212–218 (2010). College of Education, The Ohio State University

Gamification of Collaborative Learning Scenarios: Structuring Persuasive Strategies Using Game Elements and Ontologies

Geiser Chalco Challco[1], Riichiro Mizoguchi[2], Ig Ibert Bittencourt[3], and Seiji Isotani[1(✉)]

[1] ICMC, University of São Paulo, São Carlos, SP, Brazil
geiser@usp.br, sisotani@icmc.usp.br
[2] Japan Advanced Institute of Science and Technology, Nomi, Ishikawa, Japan
mizo@jaist.ac.jp
[3] Federal University of Alagoas, Maceió, Brazil
ig.ibert@ic.ufal.br

Abstract. This work presents an ontological model for the formal systematization and representation of knowledge that describes concepts from gamification and its use as Persuasive Technology (PT) in Collaborative Learning (CL) scenarios. This model enables the creation of intelligent systems that can personalize and apply the gamification techniques in group learning contexts in which the scripted collaboration decreases the motivation and engagement of students. Thus, our approach proposes to formalize the connection of concepts from theories and models to design PT in order to specify gamified CSCL scripts that induce students to willingly follow an intended learning behavior. To demonstrate the applicability of our approach, we also present a case study that shows how our ontological model could be used by in an intelligent theory-aware system to build better personalized gamified CL scenarios.

Keywords: Ontologies · Gamification · Persuasion · Persuasive strategies · Collaborative learning · CSCL scripts

1 Introduction

Despite the success in the design of Computer-Supported Collaborative Learning (CSCL) scripts to support the design of collaborative learning (CL) activities, there are situations in which these scripts may lead to demotivation [4, 6, 15]. Sometimes, a learner may neglect his personal behavior to get the task completed because he feels forced by the script and, other times, the lack of choice with respect to the sequence of activities may increase the sense of obligation. The demotivation negatively influences the learners' attitudes and behaviors, degrade group dynamics, and as a result produces long-term negative learning outcomes [6]. Thus, in recent years, the researches and practitioners are seeing gamification as a possible solution to motivate and engage the students in learning situations [11, 31].

© Springer International Publishing Switzerland 2016
F. Koch et al. (Eds.): SOCIALEDU 2015, CCIS 606, pp. 12–28, 2016.
DOI: 10.1007/978-3-319-39672-9_2

Gamification is the use of game design elements in non-game contexts [11] in which the game design theories and models are sources of verified technics, strategies and principles to gamify an scenario. One important part of these theories and models are related to the design of Persuasive Technology (PT) that focuses on the design of interactive computing products created to change peoples' attitudes and behaviors through persuasion and social influence without using coercion and/or deception [8].

The task to apply Gamification as PT to design well-thought-out gamified CL scenarios is not an easy task, in particular for an instructional designer who is a nonexpert in game design and persuasion. To do this task, it is necessary to assemble persuasive game design strategies based on deeper knowledge about principles, methods and techniques defined in the theories and models to design PT. The persuasive game design strategies are Persuasive Strategies (PSs) that consist in rules and prescriptions that define how to use the game elements for the changing of attitudes/behaviors. For example, the use of slang names in messages of a *"progress bar system"* to change the affinity of a person from *"not feeling an affinity"* to *"feeling affinity"* is a persuasive game design strategy based on the PS of suggestion.

As the attitudinal/behavioral states of persons change over time and they are dependent of a context in which the individual is in, it is necessary to look into the different PSs to decide what it is the most appropriate for each student, scenario and situation [1, 16, 23]. Nowadays, such a decision is embedded in the persuasive systems and it is realized implicitly by them, so that it only remains in the minds of designers. This fact causes difficulties in the management, modifications and evolution of PSs. Therefore, in this work, we propose an ontological model to structure and organize the PSs into the ontology **OntoGaCLeS** (an *Ontology to Gamify Collaborative Learning Scenarios*) that is available at the website: http://labcaed.no-ip.info:8003/ontogacles/.

In the following sections, we present the related works and an overview of current version of our ontology OntoGaCLeS. Next, we detail an ontological model for the conceptualization and structuration of PSs, we present a case study that describes how our proposed model can be used by an intelligent theory-aware system in the gamification of a CL scenario. Finally, the last section presents the conclusion and future work.

2 Related Works

To the best of our knowledge and by exploring different literature reviews [10, 18, 35, 36], no ontology has been proposed to offer a formal systematization of theories and models for designing PT. The search of terms *"Persuasive Technology"* and *"Ontology"* in the Scopus database returns 89 studies, of which only one study [32] proposes an ontology to represent the knowledge of literature related to human-behavior changes. This knowledge is structured in the ontology under the semantic relations and concepts of problem types, barriers, principles, strategies, mechanisms and applications. Although this ontology allows to identify PSs for solving behavior-changes problems, it is not specific for the Gamification of CL scenarios. Thus, in this study, we propose an ontological model that can be viewed as an extension of an ontology to represent behavior-change literature [32] in which we include knowledge about how the PSs must be applied using game elements.

Despite the grounding number of studies related to PT in the last years [10], and the development of many successful persuasive games, such as the HIV Roulette [8], OrderUP! [9] and Smoke? [20]; there are few generic models and frameworks to design PT, such as the Design with Intent [22] and the Persuasive System Design (PSD) model [27, 28]. Currently, the PSD model is the most complete comprising many theories and models previously developed to design PT, such as the Reasoned Action's theory [7], the Elaboration Likelihood model [30], and the Fogg's principles [8] used to define the change types of intent, the routes of persuasive messages, and the PSs, respectively. However, the PSD model lacks the information to analyze and personalize the PSs for each user. In this sense, based on the current attitudinal and behavioral states of individuals, the ontological model in this work includes structures for the representation and personalization of PSs defined in the PSD model.

In the literature, researchers and practitioners have proposed their own PSs to deal with specific problems in different contexts, such as the PSs for tailoring persuasive text messages proposed by Kaptein et al. [16], and the PSs for players of collectivist cultures developed by Khaled et al. [19]. These PSs and those that are defined in other specific frameworks and models to design PT, such as the theoretical framework of Sundar et al. [34], the model of Yusoff and Kamsin [37], and the model-driven approach of Orji, et al. [29], do not to use a set of consistent terms and vocabulary to be represented and employed by computational systems. In this sense, this work provides a common vocabulary and ontological structures that could be used to represent these PSs. Thus, a semantic web system that gives an intelligent theory-based guidance during the gamification of CL scenarios based on these PSs could be created.

3   Overview of the Ontology to Gamify CL Scenarios

Figure 1 shows the ideal flow to gamify CL scenarios from the viewpoint of an instructional designer who employs an intelligent theory-aware system based on our ontology. In the step (1), the designer sets the proper player roles and game elements for each student. In the step (2), he designs the CL gameplay as a set of CL game dynamics employing the player roles and game elements that were setting in the first phase. Finally, in the step (3), the designer makes an interaction analysis over the obtained gamified CL scenarios to propose better solutions by the meaningful result obtained during the run-time of CSCL scripts.

In previous works [2, 4, 5], we define ontological structures that allow us to accomplish the step (1) by the building of models that personalize gamification based on the individual differences of students, such as current motivation stages, psychological needs and individual personality preferences. To accomplish the step (2), the work [3] propose a set of ontological structures to represent the application of PSs in CL scenarios. To establish these structures employing concepts and semantic relations in our ontology, we use the ontology engineering techniques [24], the Hozo Ontology editor [21], and the model of roles proposed by Mizoguchi *et al.* [26].

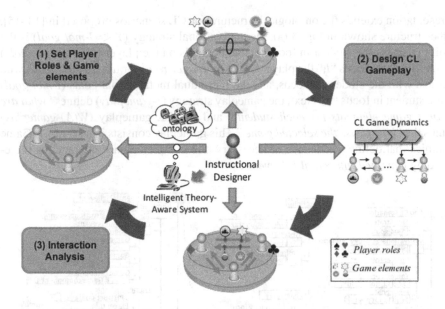

Fig. 1. Flow to gamify a CL scenario in an intelligent theory-aware system.

Thus, the current formalization of our ontology defines the terms and concepts shown in Fig. 2 (a), where *I-mot goal* is the individual motivational goal of the "person in focus" (*I*) that is to be satisfied by a motivational strategy; *I-player role* is the player defined for the person in focus (*I*); *You-player role* is the player role defined for the person (*You*) who is interacting with the person in focus (*I*); *Y <=I-mot goal* is the motivational strategy (*Y <=I-goal*) that enhances the learning strategy defined for the student in focus (*I*); *I-gameplay* is the gameplay strategy that defines the rational arrangement among player role, motivational strategy and game elements for the student in focus (*I*); and *W(A)-gameplay* is the CL gameplay that represents the interactions between students and game elements. Figure 2 (b) exemplifies a CL gameplay for the students L_A and L_B in which different game elements are setting for each student.

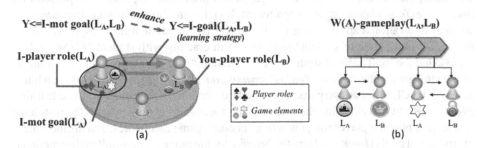

Fig. 2. (a) Terms and concepts for gamified CL scenarios; and (b) example of a CL gameplay.

Based on the concepts and terms presented above, Fig. 3 (a-d) shows the current ontological structures that we define to represent gamified CL scenarios. This representation extends the ontological structure for CL scenarios proposed in [13–15]. In the structure shown in Fig. 3 (a), the motivational strategy ($Y <=I\text{-}mot\ goal$) is the gamification for the student in focus (I) that depends on the player role ($I\text{-}player\ role$) for the student in focus "I," the player role ($You\text{-}player\ role$) for the student "You" who interacts with the student in focus, and the individual motivational goals ($I\text{-}mot\ goal$) for the student in focus "I." Next, the gameplay strategy ($I\text{-}gameplay$) defines "*what are the best game elements for each student*," and the CL gameplay ($W(A)\text{-}gameplay$) defines the "*how to use the selected game*." This gameplay consists in a set of CL Game dynamics that define a sequence of necessary and complementary interactions represented by *Gamified Influential I_L events*.

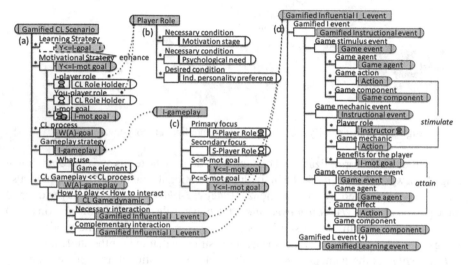

Fig. 3. Ontological structures to represent gamified CL scenarios.

The ontological structure, shown in Fig. 3 (b), allows the classification of students in different player types employing *player roles* that depend on the necessary and desire condition, such as the *motivational states, psychological needs, individual personality preferences* (e.g. playing styles, cognitive styles). Figure 3 (c) represents the *gameplay strategy* as a rational arrangement for: the player role of student in focus "*I*" (*Primary focus*), the player role of student "*You*" who is interacting with student "*I*" (*Secondary focus*), and the motivational strategy for the student "*I*" ($S <=P\text{-}mot\ goal$), the motivational strategy for the student "*You*" ($P <=mot\ goal$). Figure 3 (d) represents each interaction of CSCL script as two parts: a gamified instructional event and a gamified learning event. These two events play the role of game mechanics events, where: the instructor and learner play the player role, his actions become game mechanics, and his individual motivational goals ($I\text{-}mot\ goal$) are the *benefits for the player*. The gamified instructional and learning events also describe in a *game stimulus event* and in a *game consequence event*: the game actions that "*stimulate*" the students to do the actions defined in the instructional and learning events; and the game actions that follow the actions of students and allow them to "*attain*" their individual goals. Thus, the elements of a game event are: the "*game agents*" (e.g. point system, badge system); their "*game actions*" that stimulate the actions defined in the instructional/learning event; and their *game compo-nents* that are basic parts of game world manipulated by game agents (e.g. points, badges).

4 Conceptualization of Persuasive Game Design Strategies

The personalization of PT and Gamification have been shown effectivity to increase the motivation and engagement of users in different systems [1, 17, 29]. Our current onto-logical structures enable to represent this personalization for CSCL scripts in which the game elements are introduced to deal with the demotivation problem.

The semantic relations in the motivational strategy (*Y <=I-mot goal*) represent the dependence between the goals of CL roles and those goals of player roles that can be used to enhance a particular learning strategy. The ontological structure gameplay strategy (*I-gameplay*) reflects the personalization of game elements defined by different models of player types, so that different game elements are associated for each player role of a CL scenario. Finally, to reduce the feeling of obligation imposed by the sequencing of interactions, we represent the CL process as a sequence of gamified I_L events that represent the application of PSs using game elements for each interaction defined in a CSCL script.

The current ontological structures in our ontology does not represent the PSs them-selves, they represent the application of PSs over the sequence of interactions defined in CSCL scripts. It means that to build a model of gamification for CL scenarios, system developers have to interpret theories and models to design PT by an expert in gamifi-cation and CSCL. This interpretation only remains in their minds, causing difficulties to manage the PSs, avoiding the definition, modification and evolution of PSs. Therefore, to overcome this issue, we introduce a new stakeholder named "*Gamify Expert*" in the activity flow to gamify CL scenarios as shown in Fig. 4. We define this flow as an extension of our previous activity flow of Fig. 1 that is now defined in an in a reference architecture for semantic-web intelligent theory-aware systems.

In the new activity flow of Fig. 4, the *Gamify expert* employs a "*Gamification-framework editing environment*" to do the maintenance of PSs employing a PSs manager system that stores the PSs into a WAY-knowledge base. Next, employing an "*Intelligent theory-aware environment*" in the design of the CL gameplay, the instructional designer will find in the WAY-knowledge base for previous PSs that they have used, have expe-rienced, or have seen applied as solution in others similar scenarios or situation. After the selection of PSs, the instructional designer will be able to apply them in the CL scenario using a CL Gameplay Design Support System, following advice and recom-mendation given by this system.

To build a WAY-knowledge base that covers the different PSs, we propose to make an engineering approximation of PSs in terms of the changes in attitudinal states and behavioral states. This approximation is done in two steps. The first step is to identify the similarities and differences in the theories and models to design PT and the second step is to describe the PSs as WAY-Structures.

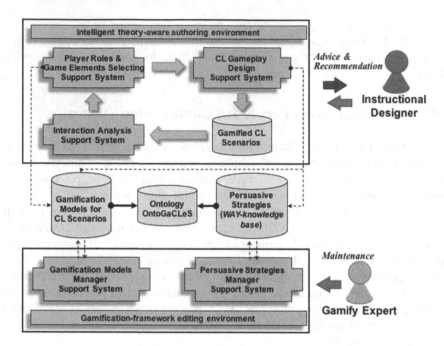

Fig. 4. Activity flow to gamify CL scenarios in a reference architecture for semantic-web intelligent theory-aware systems that will employ the ontology OntoGaCLeS

4.1 Identifying Similarities and Differences of Theories and Models to Design Persuasive Technology

The first part consists in the structuration and organization of terms, concepts and principles used in the theories and models to design PT into a set of ontological structures that define these elements as part of a whole as is shown in the nested structure of Fig. 5(a).

According to the Fig. 5(a), the gamification theories and models explain the game design process that has the purpose to obtain a plan/design of game events that will be introduced in a non-game context to gamify it. Next, the plan/design of game events is explained by theoretical justifications that have source in the game design theories and models. The purpose of the game events is to produce/induce changes in attitudinal and behavioral states of individuals in the non-game events. Finally, these changes in non-game events are explained by theories of motivation and human behavior.

Based on the nested structure mentioned above, the ontology OntoGaCLeS is categorized into the following basic concepts: Common world, Non-game world, Game world, Gamification world, as well as Theory and Model. The theories and models to design PT are defined in an ontological "*is-a*" hierarchy structure according to firstly the domains and then according to the paradigms defined in each domain. During this task, we identify the properties of theories and models, such as their principles, hypothesis, and evidences. Figure 5(b) shows part of this "*is-a*" hierarchy structure in which the concept of "*persuasive design models*" is a concept of a "*game design model.*"

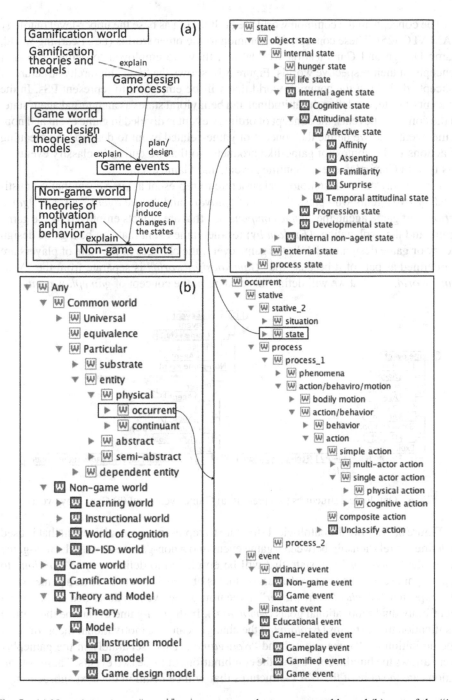

Fig. 5. (a) Nested structure of gamification, game and non-game worlds; and (b) part of the "*is-a*" hierarchy structure in the ontology OntoGaCLeS.

The concepts in the common world are built taking as base the upper-level ontology YAMATO [25]. These concepts are common to the other worlds (i.e., Learning world, Game Design and Gamification worlds) and they are employed to define particular concepts in their respective worlds. Figure 5(b) shows the "*is-a*" hierarchy structure of concepts defined in the common world that will be employed to represent PSs. In the concept of state, we define the attitudinal and behavioral states as an internal agent state. In the concept of events, the concept of ordinary event is divided in game event and non-game event, and we define the concept of game-related event to describe the meaning of actions in the context of game-like products, so that we currently classify events of this type in Gameplay event, Gamified event, and Game event.

Figure 6(a) shows the ontological structure to represent a *game event* that is consti-tuted by two agents who plays the role of "*player*" and "*game agent*," a set of "*game actions*" of game agent, the "*game components*" that are objects employed by the game agent, and the explanations (*Explain by*) for the game event that can be a game design theory or game design model. In the game event, the changes in the state of players are not defined as part of it because the "*Game design world*" is separate from the "*Non-game world*," so that we will define this change in the concept of *gameplay event*.

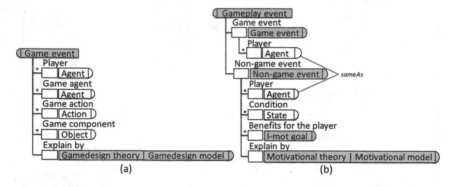

Fig. 6. Ontological structures to represent (a) Game events and (b) Gameplay events.

Figure 6(b) shows the ontological structure to represent a gameplay event that is used to define the relationship between a game event and a non-game event. In the non-game event, the "*condition*" is a state that will be employed to define: a "*precondition*" to apply a game event, and a "*terminal state*" that is obtained after to execute a game event. The expected "*benefits for the player*" in the non-game event is described employing a set of individual motivational goals (*I-mot goal*). In the non-game event, the theoretical justification that explains (*Explain by*) the changes can be a motivational theory/model. The definition of "*Game events*" and "*Non-game events*" separately in the gameplay event allows the building of various the combinations of these two events. These combi-nations are the core of the WAY-structures that will be detail in the next subsection.

4.2   Describing Persuasive Strategies as WAY-Structures

The description of PSs as WAY-structures consists in the conceptualization of ways to attain the expected changes in attitudinal and behavioral states employing a sequence of game events that influence and produce these changes. Thus, as shown in Fig. 7(a), the ontological structure *"WAY-knowledge of PS"* represents a PS as the decomposition of a macro-gameplay event into a sequence of micro-gameplay events.

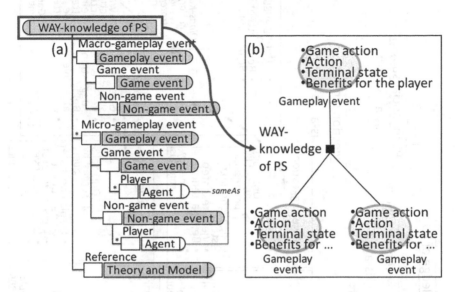

Fig. 7. (a) Ontological structure to represent a persuasive strategy; and (b) its representation as decomposition tree.

Figure 7(b) shows the representation of PS as a decomposition tree of gameplay events, where: the macro-gameplay event represents the *"what to achieve"* as a goal; and the micro-gameplay events represent the *"how to achieve"* the goal defined in the macro-event through a sequence of sub-goals. The goals in this decomposition tree for the micro- and macro-gameplay events are the *"benefits for the player"* (*I-mot goal*) or *"terminal states"* defined in the non-game events. When there are no *"benefits for the player"* in a macro-gameplay event, the goal of a decomposition tree is the *"terminal state."*

Based on the ontological structure *"WAY-knowledge of PS,"* we define a WAY-knowledge base of PSs whose part is shown in Fig. 8. In this base, the PSs are classified according to firstly the categories of PSs, and secondly according to the expected changes in the attitudinal and behavioral states. In this figure, the PS *"Oinas-Kukkonen & Harjumaa's reward strategy to increase behavior"* is defined as a *"reward strategy"* of *"PS for dialogue."* The goal of this strategy is to *"increase behavior (familiar behavior)"* making this behavior a *"familiar behavior"* (terminal state) by the action *"increase the behavior by reward."* Next, this strategy decomposes the macro-gameplay event into two micro-gameplay events that have the actions: *"measure behavior"* and *"give reward."*

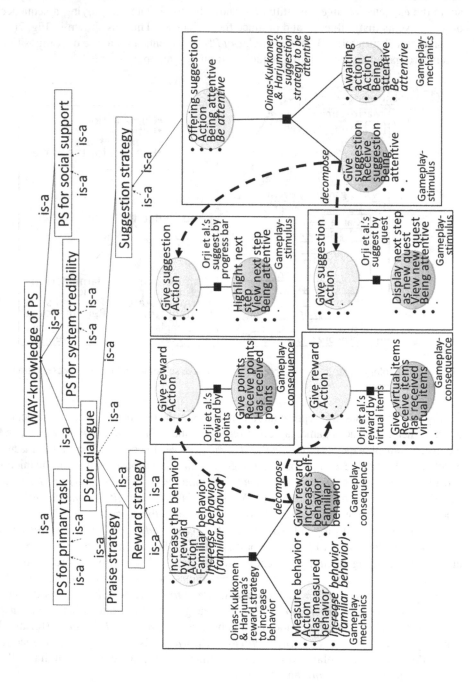

Fig. 8. A portion of the WAY-knowledge base of Persuasive Strategies.

During the action "*measure behavior*," the player performs the "*action*" defined in the macro-gameplay event, and we call this event as *gameplay-mechanics event*. After to measure behavior, in the second micro-gameplay event, the game action "*give reward*" produces the cognitive action "*increase self-behavior*" that changes the behavioral state from "*non-familiar behavior*" to "*familiar behavior*," and we call this event as *gameplay-consequence event*.

Figure 8 also shows two PSs for the decomposition of game activity "*give reward*." Both strategies are similar in the internal psychological change that they produce. However, the first PS "*Orji et al.'s reward by points*" employs a point system as a game agent to do the action "*give the points*," while the second PS "*Orji et al.'s rewards by virtual item*" employs a virtual item system as a game agent to do the action "*gives virtual items*."

Beside the reward strategy detailed above, Fig. 8 details the PS "*Oinas-Kukkonen & Harjumaa's suggestion strategy to be attentive*" defined as suggestion strategy of "*PS for dialog*." This PS decompose the macro-gameplay event with the action "*offering suggestion*" into two micro-gameplay events that have the actions: "*give suggestion*" and "*awaiting action*." In this case, for example, we show two PSs that are defined to decompose the activity "*give suggestion*," one of these strategy employs the progress bar system and the other strategy employs an "*quest system*" to do the actions "*highlight the next step*" and "*display the next step as new quest*," respectively.

5   Case Study in the CSCL Script for Argumentation

To demonstrate the utility of our approach that consists of the conceptualization of PSs presented in the previous section, we are developing an advanced authoring intelligent theory-aware system based on the reference architecture shown in Fig. 4. Figure 9 illustrates the manner in which this theory-aware system uses the WAY-knowledge base of PSs to gamify a CL scenario during the CL gameplay design. In this example, as we show in Fig. 9(a), the CL scenario being gamified is a scenario based on the CSCL script for "*argumentation, counter-argumentation and integration*" proposed by Stegmann et al. in [33]. After the selection of player roles and games elements for each student of CL scenario, as shown in Fig. 9(a-1), the socializer role is assigned for the student 11 who has the role of arguer, while the achiever role is assigned for the student 12 who has the role of co-arguer.

Figure 9(a-1) also shows that the motivational strategies for socializers and achievers are the "*Gamifying by persuasive strategy COOP*," in both cases. Figure 9(a-2) shows that the selected game elements in gameplay strategy (*I-gameplay strategy*) for socializer and achiever are the communal discovery. Finally, the individual motivation goals (*I-mot goal*) for students 12 are "*satisfy mastery*," "*be attentive*" and "*increase behavior (familiar behavior)*" as shown in Fig. 9(a-3).

The default "*CL gameplay*" for the scenario shown in Fig. 9(a-4) is obtained by employing an ontological model that extends the ontological structures shown in Fig. 3. This model employs the information defined by Orji et al. in [29], and its detail of construction can be found in [3]. As result of the application of this model, each gamified

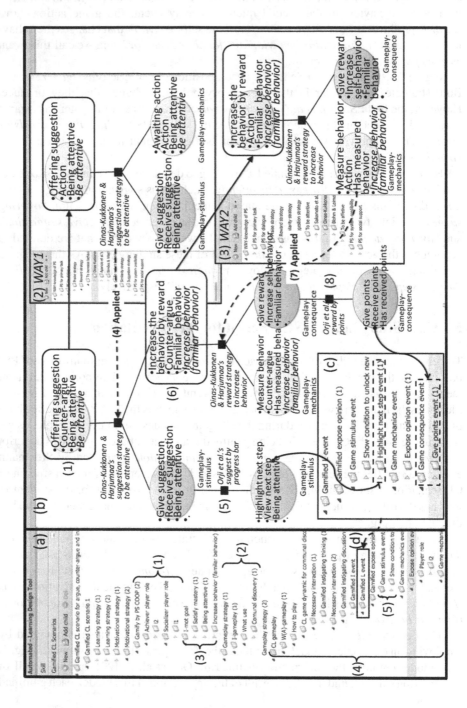

Fig. 9. Illustration of how to employ the WAY-knowledge base of Persuasive Strategies.

instructional and learning event defines the game action "*show condition to unlock new content*" as game stimulus event that persuades the student l2 to do the actions of learning event as shown in Fig. 9(a-5).

Employing the WAY-knowledge base of PSs, we can personalize the gamified instructional and learning event for each student of a gamified CL scenario by adding new game stimulus and game consequences events, so that the Fig. 9(b) shows how this personalization is done for the student l2 over the learning event "*expose opinion.*" First, after the selection of the event that will be personalized, the macro-gameplay event is automatically filled by the information of selected event as shown in Fig. 9(b-1). Based in the individual motivational goals "*be attentive*" and "*increase behavior (familiar behavior)*" of student l2, the system proposes the ways of decomposition *WAY1* and *WAY2*, respectively shown in Fig. 9(b-2) and (b-3). The first way (*WAY1*) emerges from the PS "*Oinas-Kukkonen & Harjumaa's suggestion strategy to be attentive*" because it allows to "*be attentive*" (I-mot goal). The second way (*WAY2*) emerges from the PS "*Oinas-Kukkonen & Harjumaa's reward strategy to increase behavior*" because it allows to "*increase behavior (familiar behavior).*" In this example, the designer selects the first way (*WAY1*) decomposing the macro-gameplay (Fig. 9(b-1)) into two micro-gameplay events with the game actions "*give suggestion*" and "*awaiting action*" as shown in Fig. 9(b-4). The designer can decompose the game action "*give suggestion*" by employing different PSs. For this example, the designer selects the PS "*Orji et al.'s suggest by progress bar*" as shown in Fig. 9(b-5). Next, the designer decomposes the gameplay mechanics event shown in Fig. 9(b-6) into two micro-gameplay events with the game actions "*awaiting action*" and "*give reward*" as shown in Fig. 9(b-7). This decomposition emerges from the PS "*Oinas-Kukkonen & Harjumaa's reward strategy to increase behavior*" (*WAY2*) shown in Fig. 9(b-3). Finally, the game action "*give reward*" is decomposed into the game action "give points" by the application of PS "*Orji et al.'s reward by points*" shown in Fig. 9(b-8).

The process to personalize the gamified instructional and learning event shown in Fig. 9(b) can be repeated for each student and over each instructional and learning event to define a better gamified CL scenario. At the end of this process, as shown in Fig. 9(c), the system integrates the game events in a set of game stimulus and game consequence events. For this example, the game action "*highlight next step*" done by the "*progress bar system*" is integrated into a game stimulus event, and the game action "*give points*" done by the "*point system*" is integrated in a game consequence event. Finally, the last step is the addition of game stimulus and game consequence events into its respective gamified event as shown in Fig. 9(d).

6 Conclusion and Future Steps for Our Research

In this study, we propose to structure the knowledge of PSs into the ontology *Onto-GaCLeS*. This structuration contributes to a better understanding of how to apply Gamification as PT in CL scenarios. Our approach is similar to the structuration of learning/instructional theories proposed by Hayashi *et al.* in [12]. In both cases, the theories and models are conceptualized from two viewpoints: the theory/model as a whole, and the theory/model as an aggregation of strategies. As a result of this structuration, we obtain a theory's independent and common WAY-knowledge base of PSs. Thus, we also propose a reference architecture for semantic-web intelligent theory-aware systems that employ this WAY-knowledge. Finally, to demonstrate the applicability of our approach, we illustrated the manner in which an intelligent theory-aware system based on this reference architecture allows to build better personalized gamified CL scenarios.

Our future work includes the formalization of more PSs from different theories and models to design PT, including models to design persuasive messages. We will develop a complete intelligent theory-aware system to help instructional designers in the gamification of CL scenarios. Finally, we will also evaluate the effectiveness of persuasion proposed by this system in CL scenarios.

Acknowledgements. The authors would like to thank CNPq and CAPES for supporting this research.

References

1. Busch, M., et al.: Personalization in serious and persuasive games and gamified interactions. In: Proceedings of the 2015 Annual Symposium on Computer-Human Interaction in Play, CHI PLAY 2015, pp. 811–816. ACM (2015)
2. Challco, G.C., Moreira, D.A., Bittencourt, I.I., Mizoguchi, R., Isotani, S.: Personalization of gamification in collaborative learning contexts using ontologies. IEEE Latin Am. Trans. **13**, 1995–2002 (2015)
3. Challco, G.C., Andrade, F., Oliveira, T., Mizoguchi, R., Isotani, S.: An ontological model to apply gamification as persuasive technology in collaborative learning scenarios. Anais do XXVI Simpósio Brasileiro de Informática na Educação **26**, 499–508 (2015)
4. Challco, G.C., Moreira, D.A., Mizoguchi, R., Isotani, S.: An ontology engineering approach to gamify collaborative learning scenarios. In: Baloian, N., Burstein, F., Ogata, H., Santoro, F., Zurita, G. (eds.) CRIWG 2014. LNCS, vol. 8658, pp. 185–198. Springer, Heidelberg (2014)
5. Challco, G.C., Moreira, D., Mizoguchi, R., Isotani, S.: Towards an ontology for gamifying collaborative learning scenarios. In: Trausan-Matu, S., Boyer, K.E., Crosby, M., Panourgia, K. (eds.) ITS 2014. LNCS, vol. 8474, pp. 404–409. Springer, Heidelberg (2014)
6. Falout, J., Elwood, J., Hood, M.: Demotivation: affective states and learning outcomes. System **37**, 403–417 (2009)
7. Fishbein, M., Ajzen, I.: Predicting and Changing Behavior: The Reasoned Action Approach. Psychology Press, New York (2009)
8. Fogg, B.J.: Persuasive Technology: Using Computers to Change What We Think and Do. Morgan Kaufmann, Amsterdam (2002)
9. Grimes, A., Kantroo, V., Grinter, R.E.: Let's play!: mobile health games for adults. In: Proceedings of the 12th ACM International Conference on Ubiquitous Computing, UbiComp 2010, pp. 241–250. ACM (2010)
10. Hamari, J., Koivisto, J., Pakkanen, T.: Do persuasive technologies persuade? - a review of empirical studies. In: Spagnolli, A., Chittaro, L., Gamberini, L. (eds.) PERSUASIVE 2014. LNCS, vol. 8462, pp. 118–136. Springer, Heidelberg (2014)

11. Hamari, J., Koivisto, J., Sarsa, H.: Does gamification work?–a literature review of empirical studies on gamification. In: Proceedings of the 2014 47th Hawaii International Conference on System Sciences, HICSS 2014, pp. 3025–3034. IEEE Computer Society (2014)
12. Hayashi, Y., Bourdeau, J., Mizoguchi, R.: Structuring learning/instructional strategies through a state-based modeling. In: Proceedings of the 2009 Conference on Artificial Intelligence in Education: Building Learning Systems That Care: From Knowledge Representation to Affective Modelling, pp. 215–222. IOS Press (2009)
13. Isotani, S., Mizoguchi, R., Isotani, S., Capeli, O.M., Isotani, N., de Albuquerque, A.R.: An authoring tool to support the design and use of theory-based collaborative learning activities. In: Aleven, V., Kay, J., Mostow, J. (eds.) ITS 2010, Part II. LNCS, vol. 6095, pp. 92–102. Springer, Heidelberg (2010)
14. Isotani, S., et al.: A Semantic Web-based authoring tool to facilitate the planning of collaborative learning scenarios compliant with learning theories. Comput. Educ. **63**, 267–284 (2013)
15. Isotani, S., Inaba, A., Ikeda, M., Mizoguchi, R.: An ontology engineering approach to the realization of theory-driven group formation. Int. J. Comput. Support. Collab. Learn. **4**, 445–478 (2009)
16. Kaptein, M., De Ruyter, B., Markopoulos, P., Aarts, E.: Adaptive persuasive systems: a study of tailored persuasive text messages to reduce snacking. ACM Trans. Interact. Intell. Syst. **2**, 10:1–10:25 (2012)
17. Kaptein, M., Markopoulos, P., de Ruyter, B., Aarts, E.: Personalizing persuasive technologies: Explicit and implicit personalization using persuasion profiles. Int. J. Hum Comput Stud. **77**, 38–51 (2015)
18. Kegel, R.H.P., Wieringa, R.J.: Persuasive technologies: a systematic literature review and application to PISA (2014). http://eprints.eemcs.utwente.nl/24727/01/Kegel_Wieringa_-_Persuasive_technologies%3B_a_systematic_literature_review_and_application_to_PISA.pdf
19. Khaled, R., Barr, P., Biddle, R., Fischer, R., Noble, J.: Game design strategies for collectivist persuasion. In: Proceedings of the 2009 ACM SIGGRAPH Symposium on Video Games, Sandbox 2009, pp. 31–38. ACM (2009)
20. Khaled, R., Barr, P., Boyland, J., Fischer, R., Biddle, R.: Fine tuning the persuasion in persuasive games. In: de Kort, Y.A., IJsselsteijn, W.A., Midden, C., Eggen, B., Fogg, B.J. (eds.) PERSUASIVE 2007. LNCS, vol. 4744, pp. 36–47. Springer, Heidelberg (2007)
21. Kozaki, K., Kitamura, Y., Ikeda, M., Mizoguchi, R.: Hozo: an environment for building/using ontologies based on a fundamental consideration of "Role" and "Relationship". In: Gómez-Pérez, A., Benjamins, V. (eds.) EKAW 2002. LNCS (LNAI), vol. 2473, pp. 213–218. Springer, Heidelberg (2002)
22. Lockton, D., Harrison, D., Stanton, N.A.: The Design with Intent Method: A design tool for influencing user behaviour. Appl. Ergonomics **41**, 382–392 (2010)
23. Masthoff, J., Vassileva, J.: Tutorial on personalization for behaviour change. In: Proceedings of the 20th International Conference on Intelligent User Interfaces, IUI 2015, pp. 439–442. ACM (2015)
24. Mizoguchi, R.: Tutorial on ontological engineering Part 2: Ontology development, tools and languages. New Gener. Comput. **22**, 61–96 (2004)
25. Mizoguchi, R.: YAMATO: yet another more advanced top-level ontology. In: Proceedings of the Sixth Australasian Ontology Workshop, pp. 1–16 (2010)
26. Mizoguchi, R., Sunagawa, E., Kozaki, K., Kitamura, Y.: The model of roles within an ontology development tool: hozo. Appl. Ontology Roles Interdisc. Perspect. **2**, 159–179 (2007)

27. Oinas-Kukkonen, H., Harjumaa, M.: A systematic framework for designing and evaluating persuasive systems. In: Oinas-Kukkonen, H., Hasle, P., Harjumaa, M., Segerståhl, K., Øhrstrøm, P. (eds.) PERSUASIVE 2008. LNCS, vol. 5033, pp. 164–176. Springer, Heidelberg (2008)
28. Oinas-Kukkonen, H., Harjumaa, M.: Persuasive systems design: Key issues, process model, and system features. Commun. Assoc. Inf. Syst. **24**, 28 (2009)
29. Orji, R., Vassileva, J., Mandryk, R.L.: Modeling the efficacy of persuasive strategies for different gamer types in serious games for health. User Model. User-Adap. Inter. **24**, 453–498 (2014)
30. Petty, R.E., Cacioppo, J.T.: The Elaboration Likelihood Model of Persuasion. In: Petty, R.E., Cacioppo, J.T. (eds.) Communication and Persuasion: Central and Peripheral Routes to Attitude Change. Springer Series in Social Psychology, pp. 1–24. Springer, New York (1986)
31. de Sousa Borges, S., Durelli, V.H.S., Reis, H.M., Isotani, S.: A systematic mapping on gamification applied to education. In: Proceedings of the 29th Annual ACM Symposium on Applied Computing, SAC 2014, pp. 216–222. ACM (2014)
32. Srivastava, J., Shu, L.H.: An ontology for unifying behavior-change literature. CIRP Ann. Manufact. Technol. **63**, 173–176 (2014)
33. Stegmann, K., Weinberger, A., Fischer, F.: Facilitating argumentative knowledge construction with computer-supported collaboration scripts. Int. J. Comput. Support. Collab. Learn. **2**, 421–447 (2007)
34. Sundar, S., Bellur, S., Jia, H.: Motivational technologies: a theoretical framework for designing preventive health applications. In: Bang, M., Ragnemalm, E.L. (eds.) PERSUASIVE 2012. LNCS, vol. 7284, pp. 112–122. Springer, Heidelberg (2012)
35. Torning, K.: A review of four persuasive design models. Int. J. Conceptual Struct. Smart Appl. **1**, 17–27 (2013)
36. Torning, K., Oinas-Kukkonen, H.: Persuasive system design: state of the art and future directions. In: Proceedings of the 4th International Conference on Persuasive Technology, Persuasive 2009, pp. 30:1–30:8. ACM (2009)
37. Yusoff, Z., Kamsin, A.: Game rhetoric: interaction design model of persuasive learning for serious games. In: Zaphiris, P., Ioannou, A. (eds.) LCT 2015. LNCS, vol. 9192, pp. 644–654. Springer, Heidelberg (2015)

A Full-Body Interaction Game for Children with Hearing Disabilities to Gain the Immersive Experience in a Puppet Show

Ryohei Egusa[1,2(✉)], Takahiro Nakadai[3], Tomohiro Nakayama[3], Fusako Kusunoki[4], Miki Namatame[5], Hiroshi Mizoguchi[3], and Shigenori Inagaki[2]

[1] Research Fellow of Japan Society for the Promotion of Science, Chiyoda-Ku, Tokyo, Japan
[2] Kobe University, Tsurukabuto, Nada, Kobe, Hyogo, Japan
126d103d@stu.kobe-u.ac.jp, inagakis@kobe-u.ac.jp
[3] Tokyo University of Science, Yamazaki, Noda, Chiba, Japan
{j7510085,j7513632}@ed.tus.ac.jp, hm@rs.noda.tus.ac.jp
[4] Tama Art University, Yarimizu, Hachioji, Tokyo, Japan
kusunoki@tamabi.ac.jp
[5] Tsukuba University of Technology, Amakubo, Tsukuba, Ibaraki, Japan
miki@a.tsukuba-tech.ac.jp

Abstract. In this study, we developed a full-body interaction game that assists children with hearing disabilities in experiencing a puppet show by immersing in it. The full-body interaction game presents a type of puppet show that offers opportunities for the audience to interact with the drama. It is designed so that children with hearing disabilities can participate through known communicative movements; it allows children to easily grasp how their movements affect the progress of the story. The experiment results indicate that participating children enjoy the interaction game, and that the system allows the world of the story in the puppet show seem more real.

Keywords: Puppet show · Full-body interaction · Kinect sensor · Children with hearing disabilities

1 Study Background and Purpose

A puppet show is a cultural and educational experience with which most children are acquainted [1]. Puppet shows feature interactions not found in typical animation. For example, some puppet shows include dialogue improvised between a viewer and the puppets. These interactions help add to the excitement, and draw viewers into the world of the story. However, conventional interactions in a puppet show focus mainly on verbal exchanges, and therefore tend to exclude children with hearing disabilities.

We developed a virtual puppet show system called "Interactive Puppet Theater," which is designed to increase the appreciation of children with hearing disabilities toward puppet shows [2]. The Interactive Puppet Theater has two functions. First, it converts sound information, such as letters and characters, into visual information in order to allow information delivery. The second is an interaction function operated

© Springer International Publishing Switzerland 2016
F. Koch et al. (Eds.): SOCIALEDU 2015, CCIS 606, pp. 29–38, 2016.
DOI: 10.1007/978-3-319-39672-9_3

through body motions. Children with hearing disabilities are accustomed to engaging in conversation using body language, including sign language and gestures; therefore, we predict that these children might find body movement a relatively easy and familiar mode of expression, and find the motions less taxing than attempting to use speech as a medium.

In this study, we developed a full-body interaction game that uses an interaction function to provide direct-experience-like interactions. Because the game is based on the typical motions used and experienced daily by children with hearing disabilities, we expect these children to easily grasp the game's method of operation. In addition, we aim to clarify the effects of these body motions using the full-body interaction game [3]. Therefore, this study is aimed at examining the effectiveness of the full-body interaction game for assisting children with hearing disabilities in appreciating and fully experiencing puppet shows.

2 Related Research

Children with hearing disabilities have received increasing attention in research that examines children education [4, 5]. Children with hearing disabilities often experience difficulty when acquiring information through speech; therefore, it is important to develop educational support technology for children with such disabilities. Puppet shows present a cultural and educational experience that most children have encountered; however, few studies that aim to support children with hearing disabilities have examined puppet shows.

Motion-sensing technology is gathering attention in video game research that examines player immersion and presence [6]. Playing games using body movement captured by motion-sensing technology provides not only a physical experience, but can also provide a social experience through players sharing the screen and playing space with each other [7]. In a puppet show, the social experience (e.g., sharing a single stage among the audience) is also important. Motion-sensing technology can achieve this effect without requiring the use of speech.

In addition, using body movement as a means of communication is known to effectively support children learning, including among children with hearing disabilities [8–10]; this is particularly indicated by research that examines educational immersion games that use body movement [3].

Many motion-sensing devices exist that can measure body movements and send information to computers, e.g., accelerometers, pressure sensors, and range image sensors. In specific, range image sensors are useful for measuring children body motions because they do not require the attachment of additional devices to players, and only require players to stand in view of the sensor. The Kinect (Xbox 360 Kinect Sensor, Microsoft Corporation, Redmond, WA, USA) is an especially good game-oriented input device for encouraging enjoyment, presence, and immersion [11].

3   Full-Body Interaction Game

3.1   Design

The full-body interaction game is equipped with two types of programs: ball-throwing and fan games. Both programs use the Kinect range image sensor, and body movements as the medium for communication. The Kinect sensor is used because it is known to provide immersion and enhance agreeableness in social games [12]. Figure 1 presents a system configuration diagram. The system consists of a Kinect sensor, projector, router, and two laptop computers. The body movement information obtained by the Kinect sensor is processed by the first computer; this is then sent by the router to the second computer, which converts the information into timeline-based animations. The animations respond based on this information.

The animations are displayed using the projector to form the backdrop for the puppet show. Figure 2 shows an example of the puppet show. The audience is composed of children from a prefectural elementary school for children with hearing impairments.

Both games are designed for operation using daily movements and actions. A full description is provided below; however, the following is an example from the ball-playing game: An individual brings down both of his or her arms as though throwing a large ball; consequently, an animation is displayed in the projected background that shows a ball thrown above the individual. Common and easily grasped movements are used to operate the game in order to increase its operability. Seeing their motions linked smoothly and naturally to the projected animations is intended to promote the viewers' deeper immersion in the story.

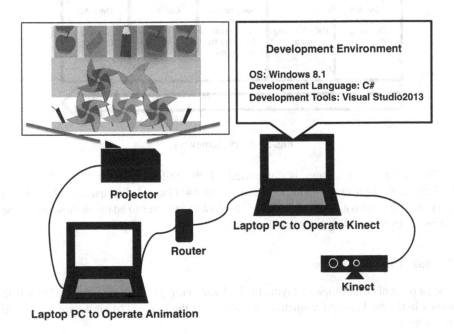

Fig. 1. System configuration

Fig. 2. Puppet show

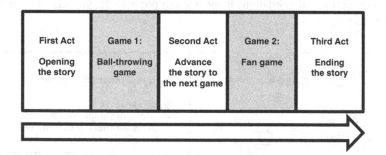

First Act	Game 1:	Second Act	Game 2:	Third Act
Opening the story	Ball-throwing game	Advance the story to the next game	Fan game	Ending the story

Fig. 3. Story framework

The puppet show's story is comprised of the following phases: (1) First Act, (2) Game 1: Ball-throwing game, (3) Second Act, (4) Game 2: Fan game, and (5) Third Act (Fig. 3). The two games are designed to allow the viewer to advance the story to the next phase by completing the game.

3.2　Ball-Throwing Game

Figure 4 presents a participant playing the ball-throwing game. In this game, a large frog appears in the background animation; the object of the game is to hit it with a ball and drive it away.

Fig. 4. Ball-throwing game

The ball-throwing game is played as follows: (a) The viewer squats on the ground and moves as though he or she were holding a large ball with both hands. (b) The viewer stands and raises both hands above his or her head. (c) He or she brings down both hands in a dramatic sweeping motion, as though throwing the ball at the frog. As the Kinect sensor detects actions (a) through (c), the viewer sees the background animations change in response. If (a) and (b) are detected, the screen falls into a hold mode where a large ball appears at the top of the animation. If (c) is detected while the screen is on hold, the ball flies toward the frog. By aiming at the frog for a set period while the system is on hold, a viewer can throw the ball at the frog and hit it; however, if the viewer throws the ball immediately from the hold position, the ball misses the frog. By hitting the frog with the ball a designated number of times, the viewer can drive away the frog, thus allowing the story to proceed to the next phase.

3.3 Fan Game

Figure 5 illustrates a viewer playing the fan game. The object of the game is to generate wind using a round paper fan in order to rotate the pinwheel in the animation to generate power.

The fan game is played as follows: First, a viewer holds a round paper fan (called "Uchiwa" in Japanese) in his or her hand, and manipulates it using a broad up-and-down motion. The Kinect sensor measures the position of the viewer's abdomen and hands; based on this measurement, the sensor counts the number of times the viewer's hands

Fig. 5. Fan game

rise above and fall below the line that designates the viewer's abdominal height. A laptop PC that operates Kinect records the number of such actions.

The background animation changes in response to the number of times this up-and-down motion is counted by the Kinect sensor. Each time one-fifth of the designated number of motions is counted, one of the five lamps shown in the background animation lights up. After all lamps are lit, power generation is achieved, and the story proceeds to the next phase.

4   Evaluation Experiment

4.1   Methods

Participants: The participants in our experiment were ten children aged 9–12 years (3rd–6th graders) from a prefectural elementary school for children with hearing impairments.

Tasks and Procedures: The participants watched a puppet show presented using the full-body interaction game. Their reactions were then examined using a questionnaire and interviews.

The questionnaire assesses subjective perceptions of the full-body interaction game using eight items; the responses use a five-point scale with the following options: "Agree very much," "Agree somewhat," "Cannot say either way," "Disagree somewhat," and "Totally disagree." The questionnaire's items are as described here. The ball-throwing game is examined using four items: "The game of hitting the ball and chasing the frog away was fun," "I was able to throw the ball exactly as I wanted," "In the game of hitting the frog with the ball and chasing it away, I felt as though I were really throwing the ball," and "By playing the game of hitting the ball and chasing the frog away, I felt like I had become a character in the story."

The fan game is also examined using four items: "The game of rotating a pinwheel with a round paper fan and creating power was fun," "I was able to rotate the pinwheel exactly as I wanted," "In the game of rotating a pinwheel with a round paper fan, I was able to feel that I was really rotating the pinwheel," and "By playing the game of rotating a pinwheel with a round paper fan and creating power, I felt like I had become a character in the story." The questionnaire items examine the effects of the full-body interaction game on the viewer's feelings about the puppet show, and the viewer's perceived ease of use of the system.

The interview survey was administered to four of the experiment participants. These were the children who participated in the story using body movements while the show was being played. The participants were asked about their experience of playing the full-body games. The interview was conducted using sign language and speech sounds to accommodate each responding child with hearing disabilities.

Study Date: The study was conducted on November 28, 2014.

4.2 Results

The questionnaire responses are divided into two categories: responses of "Agree very much" and "Agree somewhat" are deemed positive; responses of "Cannot say either way," "Disagree somewhat," and "Totally disagree" are deemed neutral/negative. Table 1 presents the results of the ball-throwing game. In all four items, there are more positive than neutral/negative responses. By calculating the direct probability of the population rate inequalities, we found a significant difference between the number of positive and neutral/negative responses for the following three items: "The game of hitting the frog with the ball and chasing it away was fun," "I was able to throw the ball exactly as I wanted," and "In the ball and frog game, I felt as though I were really throwing the ball." In contrast, the numbers of positive and neutral/negative responses for "When playing the ball and frog game, I felt like I had become a character in the story" are not significantly different.

Table 1. Questions that examine ball-throwing game.

Items	P	N
1. The game of hitting the frog with the ball and chasing it away was fun[**]	10	0
2. I was able to throw the ball exactly as I wanted[**]	9	1
3. In the ball and frog game, I felt as though I were really throwing the ball[**]	9	1
4. When playing the ball and frog game, I felt like I had become a character in the story[n.s.]	6	4

$N = 10$, [**]$p < 0.01$, [*]$p < 0.05$, [n.s.] not significant
P: Positive responses N: Neutral or Negative responses

Table 2 lists the results of the fan game. With regard to all four items, there are more positive than neutral/negative responses. By calculating the direct probability of the population rate inequalities, we found a significant difference between the number of positive and negative responses for the following three items: "The game of rotating the pinwheel with a round paper fan and generating power was fun," "I was able to rotate the pinwheel exactly as I wanted," and "In the fan game, I was able to feel that I was really rotating the pinwheel." In contrast, the numbers of positive and negative responses for "When playing the fan game, I felt like I had become a character in the story" are not significantly different.

Table 2. Questions that examine fan game

Items	P	N
5. The game of rotating the pinwheel with a round paper fan and generating power was fun[**]	10	0
6. I was able to rotate the pinwheel exactly as I wanted[*]	8	2
7. In the fan game, I was able to feel that I was really rotating the pinwheel[**]	9	1
8. When playing the fan game, I felt like I had become a character in the story[n.s.]	7	3

$N = 10$, [**]$p < 0.01$, [*]$p < 0.05$, [n.s.] not significant
P: Positive responses N: Neutral or Negative responses

Tables 3 and 4 are representative of the majority of responses with regard to the full-body games. Table 3 presents the responses from subject 1 (hereafter referred to as S1) with regard to the enjoyment of the full-body games. S1 stated, "I enjoyed the ball-throwing game and... game of paper round fun [fun game]" (sic). An experimenter (hereafter referred to as E) enquired about S1's reasons; S1 replied, "My body felt warm." We consider that playing games using body movement brought S1 enjoyment and excitement.

Table 3. Response samples with regard to enjoyment of full-body interaction games

Speaker	Transcript
E:	Please, let us know about your experience watching the puppet show.
S1:	I enjoyed the ball-throwing game and... game of paper round fun [fun game].
E:	Did you enjoy it?
S1:	Yes.
E:	What makes you think so?
S1:	Mmm... I ... My body felt warm.
E:	You moved your body and felt warm?
S1:	[Nodding]

E: Experimenter; S1: Subject 1

Table 4. Response samples with regard to immersion in full-body interaction games

Speaker	Transcript
E:	Please, let us know about your experience watching the puppet show.
S2:	I had fun.
E:	Did you have fun?
S2:	[Nodding]
E:	Why did you enjoy it?
S2:	I played games. I felt actually that I play [throwing balls and rotate pinwheel with paper round fun]. [omission]
E:	Did you enjoy playing games with body movements?
S2:	I feel a little tired, but I enjoyed those.

E: Experimenter; S2: Subject 2

Table 4 presents the responses of subject 2 (hereafter referred to as S2) with regard to the full-body games' immersion. S2 said, "I played games. I felt actually that I played [throwing balls and rotate pinwheel with paper round fun]" (sic). Afterward, S2 said, "I feel a little tired, but I enjoyed those [full-body interaction games]." We consider that full-body interaction helped S2 become immersed in, and enjoy, the puppet show.

5   Conclusion

The results indicate that the full-body interaction game was effective with regard to the participants' fun, ease of use, and sense of reality. The participants in our experiment reported that the full-body interaction game provided direct-experience-like interactions while watching the puppet show. The rates of positive and neutral/negative responses to questions about personal participation ("I felt like I had become a character in the story") were not significantly different between the two types of full-body interaction games.

Our results suggest that children with hearing disabilities can experience the full-body interaction game as fun and easy to use. In addition, it can provide children with a sense of the world evoked in puppet shows. These findings suggest that experience-type of interactions with full-body interaction games allow participants to become deeply immersed in puppet shows. Nonetheless, more detailed investigation is required to clarify why no significant differences were detected in the participants' feelings of personal participation.

Acknowledgments. This work was supported by Grant-in-Aid for JSPS Fellows Number 15J00608 and JSPS KAKENHI Grant Number 26282061.

References

1. Hunt, T., Renfro, N.: Puppetry in Early Childhood Education. Nancy Renfro Studios, Austin (1982)
2. Egusa, R., Wada, K., Adachi, T., Goseki, M., Namatame, M., Kusunoki, F., Mizoguchi, H., Inagaki, S.: Evaluation of interactive puppet theater based on inclusive design methods: a case study of students at elementary school for the deaf. In: Proceedings of the 12th International Conference on Interaction Design and Children, pp. 467–470. ACM, New York (2013)
3. Adamo-Villani, N., Wright, K. SMILE: An immersive learning game for deaf and hearing children. In: Proceedings of ACM SIGGRAPH 2007 Educators Program, article no. 17. ACM, San Diego (2007)
4. Lee, S., Henderson, V., Hamilton, H., Starner, T., Brasher, H: A gesture-based american sign language game for deaf children. In: Proceedings of CHI 2005 Extended Abstracts on Human Factors in Computing Systems, pp. 1589–1592. ACM, Portland (2005)
5. Gentry, M.M., Chinn, K.M., Moulton, R.D.: Effectiveness of multimedia reading materials when used with children who are deaf. Am. Ann. Deaf **149**(5), 394–403 (2005). Gallaudet University Press, Washington, DC, USA
6. McMahan, A.: Immersion, engaging, presence, a method for analyzing 3-D video games. In: Wolf, M.J.P., Perron, B. (eds.) The Video Game, Theory Reader, pp. 67–86. Routledge, Taylor & Francis Group, New York (2003)
7. Eisenberg, M., Pares, N.: Tangible and full-body interfaces in learning. In: Sawyer, R.K. (ed.) The Cambridge Handbook of the Learning Science, pp. 339–357. Cambridge University Press, New York (2014)
8. Klemmer, S.R., Hartmann, B., Takayama, L.: How bodies matter: five themes for interaction design. In: DIS 2006 Proceedings of the 6th Conference on Designing Interactive Systems, pp. 140–149. ACM, University Park (2006)
9. Kynigos, C., Smyrnaiou, Z., Roussou, M.: Exploring rules and underlying concepts while engaged with collaborative full-body games. In: Proceedings of the 9th International Conference on Interaction Design and Children, pp. 222–225. ACM, Barcelona (2010)
10. Abrahamson, D.: The monster in the machine, or why educational technology needs embodied design. In: Lee, V. (ed.) Learning Technologies and the Body, pp. 21–38. Routledge, Taylor & Francis Group, New York (2015)
11. Shafer, D.M., Carbonara, C.P., Popova, L.: Spatial presence and perceived reality as predictors of motion-based video game enjoyment. Presence **20**(6), 591–619 (2011). MIT Press, Massachusetts, USA
12. Birk, M., Mandryk, R.L.: Control your game-self: effects of controller type on enjoyment, motivation, and personality in game. In: CHI 2013 Proceedings of the SIGCHI Conference on Human Factors in Computing System, pp. 685–694. ACM, Paris (2013)

A Learning Object Recommendation Model with User Mood Characteristics

Néstor Darío Duque Méndez[1]([⊠]), Ángela María Pérez Zapata[1],
and Cesar A. Collazos[2]

[1] Universidad Nacional de Colombia Sede Manizales, Manizales, Colombia
{ndduqueme,amperezz}@unal.edu.co
[2] Universidad del Cauca, Popayán, Colombia
ccollazo@unicauca.edu.co

Abstract. Emotions influence human cognition, affecting perception and understanding of a specific situation; therefore emotions can affect positively or negatively the learning process. Currently there are few information systems that analyze users' emotions to optimize their learning. This article proposes a model that includes users' temporary emotions to recommend Learning Objects (LO) and deliver relevant educational materials. Three stages are set; initially, the model recognizes a user's emotions and learning style; then a recommendation system is applied to identify relevant LOs; and finally, the presentation of this information is showed to the user. In this work we present a method that identifies the emotion of the user based on facial recognition, and the process of recommendation is presented.

Keywords: Mood recommender systems · Learning object recommendation · Affective recommender

1 Introduction

Recommender systems are important in educational environment as they allow users to get educational resources that meet their needs or interests. But as other characteristics that guide recommendation appear, the systems become more complex and the difficulty of obtaining some values becomes a problem to solve. A particular case is related to user's recognize emotions and their relationship with the custom recovery processes. This issue is related to the principles of affective computing, which is a field of artificial intelligence that gives a computer the ability to recognize, interpret, process and express emotions [1].

The role of emotions in the learning process is studied, generating improvements to this experience. [2] proposes an experimental prototype that provides educational materials to students according to their emotional states, generating a 91 % increase in their learning performance. Recognition of user emotions to interact in educational settings is a challenge to implement due that emotions change over the time. But it is necessary to monitor in a permanent way the mood of the student, allowing identifying the relationship between emotions and learning for future recommendations.

© Springer International Publishing Switzerland 2016
F. Koch et al. (Eds.): SOCIALEDU 2015, CCIS 606, pp. 39–48, 2016.
DOI: 10.1007/978-3-319-39672-9_4

A recommendation model for digital educational resources based on learning style and user temporary emotions is proposed. The aim of this work is to improve the relevance of educational material delivered, looking for a positive impact on the learning process. The model proposed is composed by three stages: user model capture, recommendation module and presentation module. Because the complexity of identifying the user mood, some alternatives are presented.

In the next section, some concepts and related work are presented. Then, in Sect. 3, a first approach of the overall proposal and finally, conclusions and future work are depicted.

2 Theoretical Aspects and Related Works

The emotions are a great influence on human cognition [3]. But the emotions are a difficult concept to define; there are many results with different approaches, which hinders the accuracy of the identification and representation of these emotions by computers [4]. According to the Royal Spanish Academy emotion is defined as "intense and fleeting disturbance, pleasant or painful, which is accompanied by certain somatic shock", where "the mood" is interpreted as the perception people have of emotions, and "somatic shock" refers to physical manifestations that can generate human emotions; These two factors are essential in identifying emotions through the computer, where the affective computing derived from the Artificial Intelligence, whose main objective is to develop computational methods aimed at recognizing and generate human emotions [1], is an important aspect.

Recommendation systems mainly aim to provide users the closest and best needs adapted searching results, making predictions about their preferences and showing those items that best fit to what users expect [5].

The most used techniques in the various recommendation systems identified are: collaborative, allowing identify similarities with other users and to recommend the elements delivered before; the demographic recommendation classified and recommended by groups from users, based on content uses user profile and is related with the characteristics of the element to recommend, based on history or in the knowledge where the element type is associated with past decisions of users. The hybrid techniques [6], allow complement each other, and its use take advantage of both benefits.

In [7], an Educational Recommender System, is presented. The aim of this article is to present a student-centered Learning Object (LO) recommender system based on a hybrid recommendation technique that combines the three following approaches: content-based, collaborative and knowledge-based. In addition, those LO adapted to the student profile are retrieved from LO repositories using the stored descriptive metadata of these objects.

In [8], authors modify the traditional collaborative-filtering based recommendation approach by injecting user mood and proposed a mood-aware collaborative-filtering approach. This study includes 16 mood states in three categories: positive, negative and others, based on the commonly adopted PANAS-X mood inventory. Empirical studies demonstrate that the mood-aware recommendation approach performs better than the traditional one, which does not consider mood [9].

In [10], a novel framework for emotion-based music recommendation is proposed. The core of the recommendation framework is the construction of the music emotion model by affinity discovery from film music, which plays an important role in conveying emotions in film. An experimental result shows that the proposed emotion-based music recommendation achieves 85 % accuracy in average.

In [2], an affective model of emotional states where the users were related to the profile and object of learning is presented. But required biosensors and learning objects based on knowledge. Limiting the model to receive biophysical signals to identify the emotion, and perform recommendation for learning self-rhythmic. Moreover, [11] proposes a four activities methodology using methods of user-centered design and data mining techniques requiring large processing capabilities. In addition webcam is required to analyze the facial expression of the user to identify the emotion.

3 Proposal

From the previous section it is clear that affective computing allow identify and analyze the emotional state of the user in order to obtain the type of educational resource that could be adapted to the student according its permanent and non-permanent features. This article proposes a model, shown in Fig. 1, which has three stages; each of one can have variations in approaches and techniques to implement.

3.1 First Stage

It is required to determine the learning style and mood of the student. There are different proposals for users' classification, according to learning styles and various instruments for measurement. Initially, for example, it must make learning style obtained by Felder Test [12].

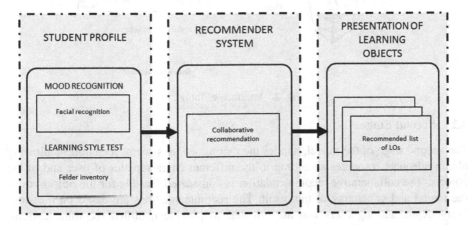

Fig. 1. Recommendation model focused on emotions, seeking to optimize the learning effect on users.

For user's emotional state recognition, different methods can be applied: directly asking users what their mood is a simple mechanism; perform specialized tests to determine different variables related to mood, including PANAS, or expanded PANASX [9] version; apply voice or text recognition algorithms [13], or facial expressions recognition, using specialized devices that allow monitoring physical changes by physiological signals, too blood pressure measurement, measurement of skin conductance, heart rate identifying their changes or verifying pupil diameter, etc. [14, 15]. The model has the possibility of expanding or combine these methods, for obtaining the mood, trying to improve recognition accuracy.

For this proposal, the values assigned to each category of the learning styles correspond to those set in the Felder Inventory [12], which are the odd numbers between −11 and 11; therefore, for the first category, which is active/reflective, a value of 9 would indicate that the student has a more reflexive tendency.

On the other hand, the mood values are obtained by *eMotion software*, developed by ISLA Lab of Amsterdam University. It provides a Java demo version, allowing recognition of the user face to identify automatically and in real time, the mood, through some specific features. This application is able to recognize seven moods: neutral, happiness, surprise, angry, disgust, fear and sadness. eMotion represents the amount of moods that the user can feel through a percentage, allowing the identification of the existence of a main mood.

Figure 2 shows the interface of eMotion.

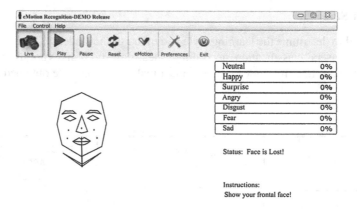

Fig. 2. Interface eMotion.

3.2 Second Stage

The second stage of the model, applies the recommender systems techniques, allowing obtain adequate resources according to the different characteristics of user and of the objects. The collaborative recommendation is considered feasible for the objectives of the model and generating of the result. The recommendations are based on the similarity degree among users and are oriented to provide qualified recommendations, aiming suggest new items or predicting the utility of a certain item for a particular user, based on the choices of other similar users.

Felder learning style and mood values obtained from the recognition module are characteristics to be assessed for getting the k-neighbors.

The recommendation is made through collaborative filtering, searching for a similar profile to the user who is doing the request, to deliver an educational resource evaluated positively [16].

Cosine Distance calculation is usually used with vectors, whose elements are numeric values and is required mathematical operations on such elements. The cosine similarity between two vectors is a measure that calculates the cosine of the angle between them. This metric is a measurement of orientation and not magnitude; it can be seen as a comparison among data on a normalized space. What we have to do to build the cosine similarity equation is to solve the equation of the dot product for the cosine; the calculation is done by the Formula 1:

$$\text{Cosine Similarity } S(\mathbf{X}, \mathbf{Y}) = \sum\nolimits_{i=1}^{n} (X_i \cdot Y_i) \bigg/ \sqrt{\left(\sum\nolimits_{i=1}^{n} X_i^2 \cdot \sum\nolimits_{i=1}^{n} Y_i^2 \right)} \quad (1)$$

Where, $\mathbf{X}$ and $\mathbf{Y}$ are vectors of characteristics of students, by example.

3.3   Three Stage

The recommendation process starts from the search criteria (keywords or educational skills to be achieved).

In phase 3, the system provides a list of recommended items, according to the learning style and mood and according to the results of similar students.

4   Validation

The validation was performed with learning objects stored in FROAC (Federation of Learning Object Repositories - Colombia); performing an initial search with the word "algoritmos" for selecting LO that were to process. Figure 3 show the output from FROAC.

Collaborative Filtering Recommendation is a method of making automatic predictions the objects that had been evaluated by students with similar profiles. The algorithm used for similarity is the cosine metric.

The first step is make learning style test, through by Felder Inventory, and recognition of the user's emotional state through eMotion.We worked with a group of 20 computer science students.

Table 1 shows the results obtained with Felder Inventory for the first 5 students. Table 2 shows the results obtained with the *eMotion* software for the first 5 students. The data have been grouped into positive (average of values of happy and surprise), negative (average of values of angry, fear, disgust and sad) and neutral mood, based on [9].

Table 3 integrates the data of learning style and mood, taken to a group of students when making queries and then stored in the system. These data are the basis for

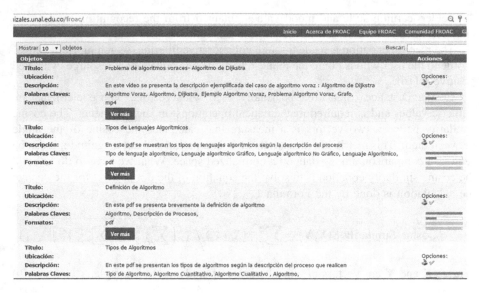

Fig. 3. FROAC output.

Table 1. Students' learning styles

Reflective	Intuitive	Verbal	Global
1	3	7	−3
−9	−1	7	11
−9	−1	7	11
−9	−1	7	11
9	11	7	−7

Table 2. Students'Mood data

Percentage Data										
Neut	Happy	Surp	Angr	Disg	Fear	Sad	Total	Positive	Negative	Neutral
35	0	0	28	0	1	35	99	0	16	35
0	0	0	0	96	0	4	100	0	25	0
0	100	0	0	0	0	0	100	50	0	0
0	0	0	51	2	0	47	100	0	25	0
0	0	83	1	0	2	13	99	41	4	0

obtaining similarity with other users and to make the recommendation process. In order to make possible the calculations, the data have been normalized between 0–5, as shown in Table 3.

Table 3. Data obtained for students for the experiment.

Id	Active/Reflective	Sensory/Intuitive	Visual/Verbal	Sequential/Global	Positive	Negative	Neutral
1	2,73	3,18	4,09	1,82	0,00	0,80	1,75
2	0,45	2,27	4,09	5,00	0,00	1,25	0,00
3	0,45	2,27	4,09	5,00	2,50	0,00	0,00
4	0,45	2,27	4,09	5,00	0,00	1,25	0,00
5	4,55	5,00	4,09	0,91	2,08	0,20	0,00
6	0,45	2,27	4,09	5,00	0,00	0,10	4,60
7	3,18	3,64	1,82	4,55	0,08	1,11	0,40
8	0,45	2,27	4,09	5,00	0,10	1,19	0,00
9	3,18	3,64	1,82	4,55	2,33	0,09	0,00
10	4,55	1,36	0,91	3,64	0,68	0,90	0,00
11	0,45	2,27	4,09	5,00	0,00	0,09	4,65
12	2,73	3,18	4,09	1,82	0,38	1,06	0,00
13	2,73	3,18	4,09	1,82	0,00	1,25	0,00
14	4,55	1,36	0,91	3,64	0,00	1,25	0,00
15	0,45	2,27	4,09	5,00	2,05	0,23	0,00
16	4,09	0,00	0,00	0,91	1,70	0,40	0,00
17	2,73	3,18	4,09	1,82	0,00	1,25	0,00
18	2,73	3,18	4,09	1,82	0,00	1,24	0,00
19	4,55	1,36	0,91	3,64	2,00	0,25	0,00
20	2,73	3,18	4,09	1,82	0,05	1,23	0,00

To validate the proposal, a test was performed with a student "Y" with the profile showed in Table 4.

Table 4. Student data case study"Y".

Id	Active/Reflective	Sensory/Intuitive	Visual/Verbal	Sequential/Global	Positive	Negative	Neutral
Y	2,73	3,18	4,09	1,82	0,00	0,80	1,75

With the students registered in Table 3, some searches had been conducted related to the word "algoritmos" and the students classified the recovered object as relevant or not. The proposed system must recommend the student "Y" the objects, according to similarity with other students.

Table 5 presents the results according to Formula 1. We have highlighted the five most similar to the student "Y" (id 5, 12 and 20).

With the results of the search, the students were asked to rate the first 10 objects delivered by the system according to their quick perception. The identifiers of these objects are: 197, 20, 17, 18, 57,65,66,64, 63, and 87.

Table 6 reflects the ratings by the users involved in the experiment, showing the objects qualified as relevant. On the other hand, the objects relevant according to the student "Y" were 197, 17, 18, 57 and 65.

The column precision, is the fraction of cases retrieved from the student "i", which are relevant to the student "Y"; that corresponds to the fraction of positive predictions which are correct.

Table 5. The Cosine Similarity of students with student "Y".

ID	S(X,Y)	ID	S(X,Y)
1	0,9066254	11	0,62633256
2	0,75723791	**12**	**0,95761016**
3	0,82254761	13	0,93663014
4	0,75723791	14	0,65932233
5	**0,95861173**	15	0,82016048
6	0,62855669	16	0,53752332
7	0,78774742	**17**	**0,93663014**
8	0,7623753	**• 18**	**• 0,9368475**
9	0,8482015	19	0,72978353
10	0,69359719	**20**	**0,93966156**

Table 6. Data of the experiment and Precision.

Student	LO (+)Student "i"	LO (+)Student "Y"	Precision metric
1	197, 20, 17, 18,57, 65	197,17, 18, 57, 65	0,833
2	20, 18,65, 64	197,17, 18, 57, 65	0,500
3	20, 18,65, 64,66	197,17, 18, 57, 65	0,400
4	20, 17,18,57, 65, 64,66	197,17, 18, 57, 65	0,571
5	197, 17, 18, 57, 65	197,17, 18, 57, 65	1,000
6	20, 18,65, 64,66	197,17, 18, 57, 65	0,400
7	197, 20, 17, 18, 57	197,17, 18, 57, 65	0,800
8	18,65, 64,66	197,17, 18, 57, 65	0,500
9	20, 18,65, 64	197,17, 18, 57, 65	0,500
10	17, 18, 57, 65	197,17, 18, 57, 65	1,000
11	20, 65, 64,66	197,17, 18, 57, 65	0,250
12	17, 18, 57	197,17, 18, 57, 65	1,000
13	20, 18,57, 65, 64,66	197,17, 18, 57, 65	0,500
14	197, 18, 57, 65	197,17, 18, 57, 65	1,000
15	18,65, 64,66	197,17, 18, 57, 65	0,500
16	17, 18, 57, 65	197,17, 18, 57, 65	1,000
17	197, 17, 18, 65	197,17, 18, 57, 65	1,000
18	17, 18, 57,66	197,17, 18, 57, 65	0,750
19	17, 18, 57, 65	197,17, 18, 57, 65	1,000
20	17, 18, 57	197,17, 18, 57, 65	1,000

Precision is then defined as:

$$Precision = \frac{tp}{tp + fp} \qquad (2)$$

Where tp are common results with previous users, and fp the number of objects not relevant by the user of the experiment.

For student 5, the highest similarity with the student "Y" is:

$$Precision = \frac{5}{5+0} = 1,000$$

As it is depicted in Table 6, without being conclusive, mood could influences the rating of the selected learning objects. The results could evidence that there is influence on the decisions, modifying the user behavior in this time slot generating an additional element in the recommendation. Precision for the students with more similar profile have been placed in highlighted (id 5,12, 17, 18 and 20) and in several of them, the precision measurements are good (1,000). But some precision measurements with identical value are referred to students with poor similarity. This is due in part to the evaluation of objects was a quick perception and does not influence some characteristics related to learning style, which is more associated to the way we process information in the learning process. Other metrics, as accuracy, would deliver less satisfactory results, because there are false negatives fn.

5   Conclusions and Further Work

The recommendation systems hold promise in learning process not only for their purposes of helping learners and educators to find useful resources, but also as a means of bringing together people with similar interests.

The importance of the student emotional state on the results of the different educational activities requires that the systems can adapt to these conditions. The problem is associated with the changing conditions of the emotions and the possibilities of detecting these changes for the system to reconfigure adaptively.

The work presented is a first approach to the application of the proposed model; it was validated to explore the possibility of linking the components of the 3 phases, with encouraging results.

As future work is to theoretically and technically strengthen each phase, implement the proposed variants and test the system in a real environment. In addition to assessing the specific impact on the effectiveness of the educational process. On the other hand, implement hybrid recommendations and evaluate the results.

Acknowledgements. The research reported in this paper was funded in part by the COL-CIENCIAS Project entitled "RAIM: Implementación de un framework apoyado en tecnologías móviles y de realidad aumentada para entornos educativos ubicuos, adaptativos, accesibles e interactivos para todos" Universidad Nacional de Colombia, with code 111956934172.

References

1. Picard, R.: Affective Computing. MIT Press, Cambridge (1997)
2. Shen, L., Wang, M., Shen, R.: Affective e-learning: using emotional data to improve learning in pervasive learning environment. J. Educ. Technol. Soc. **12**(2), 176–189 (2009)

3. Tejedor,A.B., Andoni, C.M.: Inteligencia y Educación Emocional (2009)
4. Lei, J., Rao, Y., Li, Q., Quan, X., Wenyin, L.: Towards building a social emotion detection system for online news. Future Gener. Comput. Syst. **37**, 438–448 (2014)
5. Mizhquero, K.: Análisis, Diseño e Implementación de un Sistema Adaptivo de Recomendación de Información Basado en Mashups. In: Rev. Tecnológica ESPOL (2009)
6. Rodríguez, P., Duque, N., Ovalle, D.A.: Multi-agent system for knowledge-based recommendation of learning objects using metadata clustering. In: Bajo, J., et al. (eds.) PAAMS 2015 Workshops. CCIS, vol. 524, pp. 356–364. Springer, Heidelberg (2015)
7. Rodríguez, P.A., Ovalle, D.A., Duque, N.D.: A student-centered hybrid recommender system to provide relevant learning objects from repositories. In: Zaphiris, P., Ioannou, A. (eds.) LCT 2015. LNCS, vol. 9192, pp. 291–300. Springer, Heidelberg (2015)
8. Winoto, P., Tang, T.: The role of user mood in movie recommendations. Expert Syst. Appl. **37**(8), 6086–6092 (2010)
9. Watson, D., Clark, L.A.: THE PANAS-X manual for the positive and negative affect schedule - expanded form. Order A J. Theory Ordered Sets Appl. **277**(6), 1–27 (1994)
10. Shan, M.-K., Kuo, F.-F., Chiang, M.-F., Lee, S.-Y.: Emotion-based music recommendation by affinity discovery from film music. Expert Syst. Appl. **36**(4), 7666–7674 (2009)
11. Santos, O.C.; Saneiro, M.; Salmeron-Majadas, S.; Boticario, J.G.: A methodological approach to eliciting affective educational recommendations. In: Advanced Learning Technologies, pp. 529–533 (2014)
12. Felder, R.M., Spurlin, J.: Applications, reliability and validity of the index of learning styles. Int. J. Eng. Educ. **21**(1), 103–112 (2005)
13. Li, W., Xu, H.: Text-based emotion classification using emotion cause extraction. Expert Syst. Appl. **41**(4), 1742–1749 (2014)
14. Sano, A., Picard, R.W.: Stress recognition using wearable sensors and mobile phones. In: 2013 Humaine Association Conference on Affective Computing and Intelligent Interaction, pp. 671–676 (2013)
15. Webb, R.C., Pielak, R.M., Bastien, P., Ayers, J., Niittynen, J., Kurniawan, J., Manco, M., Lin, A., Cho, N.H., Malyrchuk, V., Balooch, G., Rogers, J.A.: Thermal transport characteristics of human skin measured in vivo using ultrathin conformal arrays of thermal sensors and actuators. PLoS ONE **10**(2), e0118131 (2015)
16. Vekariya, V., Kulkarn, G.R.: Hybrid recommender systems: survey and experiments. In: Second International Conference on Digital Information and Communication Technology and it's Applications (DICTAP), pp. 469–473 (2012)

A Quantitative Analysis of Learning Objects and Their Metadata in Web Repositories

Andre Luiz da Costa Carvalho[1(✉)], Moises G. de Carvalho[1], Davi Guimaraes[1],
Davi Kalleb[1], Roberto Cavalcanti[1], Rodrigo S. Gouveia[1], Helvio Lopes[1],
Tiago T. Primo[2], and Fernando Koch[2]

[1] Instituto de Computação, Universidade Federal do Amazonas, Manaus, Brazil
{andre,moises,daviiitb,dkmsilva,rccn,rsg,hlon}@icomp.ufam.edu.br
[2] Samsung Research Institute Brazil, Campinas, Brazil
{thiago.t,fernando.koch}@samsung.com

Abstract. This work conducts a quantitative analysis of a number of Learning Object Repositories (LORs) of Learning Objects (LOs) in both English and Portuguese languages. The focus of this exercise is to understand how the contributors organize their metadata, the update frequency, and measurement upon LOR items such as: (i) the size distribution; (ii) growth rate, and; (iii) statistics about metadata completion, blank fields and LO types. We conclude our analysis with a discussion about the implications of our findings upon tasks such as LO search and recommendation.

1 Introduction

Learning Objects (LOs) are digital assets that can be used to assist the learning process of a subject. Any piece of electronic content that can provide information to support educational activities can be considered a LO [10,12,22]. They are usually stored in large repositories designed to support educational activities (refereed as Learning Object Repositories - LORs) [10,14] that can benefit on the use of computers or similar devices, such as tablets or smartphones, to provide access to its contents.

The main idea behind Learning Objects is to break the educational content into smaller pieces that can be reused in several different educational environments [22]. They can be found in different encodings, such as images, texts, videos, audios, games, animations, interactive simulations, tests, etc., and can be seen as pieces that can be combined and used to enrich educational activities, supported by computers and other digital capable devices. For example, one teacher can combine an animation of the earth orbiting around the sun with a description text in a class on the "gravity" subject.

The growing utilization of Digital Teaching Platforms (DTP) [6] lead to a demand for LOs for the composition of complex digital education content. The focus of the next generation of tablet-centric digital education [9] is to promote methods to enhance student engagement that will consequently lead to

F. Koch et al. (Eds.): SOCIALEDU 2015, CCIS 606, pp. 49–64, 2016.
DOI: 10.1007/978-3-319-39672-9_5

an increase of overall learning performance [3]. One of the key factors in implementing DTP is to make use of elaborated digital content to enhance technology acceptability by both teacher and student. This is one step towards the ideal of engagement enhancement. For that, there is an increasingly demand for LORs able to provide digital content suitable to tablet-centric computing and organized in such a way that facilitates content search and automated recommendation.

Thus, this work presents a quantitative analysis of a number of web LORs, regarding both its LO creation as well as its metadata, in order to better understand the present situation of LORs to provide useful information for future works intending to use their data. We present updated information regarding the LOs, along with an analysis of the state of the metadata describing the LOs in the different repositories. This is an innovative approach when characterizing a large number of LORs.

In order to harness the power of LOs in an educational environment, and to create tools to facilitate the finding and use of LOs by educators, such as recommender systems and advanced search interfaces, first it is essential to understand exactly how those LOs are organized in the repositories. While in theory every LO in every repository has a bulky amount of metadata giving the best descriptions possible for each LO, in reality each repository is its own distinct beast. Despite the existence of metadata standards and ontologies, much of the time repositories using the same standard might have vastly different metadata description practices between their contributors, or even almost to no metadata at all.

In this environment, the decision of keeping LORs with "dirty" data (i.e., with replicas, with no standardized representation, several different metadata standards, incomplete descriptions, etc.) goes far beyond technical questions such as the overall speed or performance of data management systems. The solutions available for addressing this problem require more than technical efforts, they need management and cultural changes as well [21].

There has been a large investment from private and government organizations in the development of methods for cleaning and removing replicas from data repositories [2, 21]. The problem of detecting and removing duplicate entries in a repository is generally known as record deduplication [4]. In the specific scenario of the LORs, a successful deduplication process eases further data handling and integration related tasks, such as search and recommendation services.

In our analysis, we collected the metadata related to 905,878 LOs stored in 30 different LORs (both international and Brazilian). With our analysis, we want not only to try to find general characteristics in common of the different LORs, but also to create an information profile of the major distinct characteristics found in each LOR. These profiles can be useful, for instance, for data cleaning and integration tasks, which are essential for applications that intend to use information from extracted from more than a single distinct LOR.

This work is organized as follows. In Sect. 2 we review the related work. In Sect. 3 we briefly introduce the major LO metadata description standards we found. In Sect. 4 we present the major characteristics of the LORs and the information profile we have build for each one of them. The work concludes with directions and recommendation for future work in Sect. 5.

2 Related Work

Reusing the same content for different educational activities is the key concept for the adoption of Learning Objects. However, there are several LO metadata standards, which are used by several different LORs. This scenario creates a problem for integration and reuse efforts, as well as any effort to use this data in an integrated fashion.

The authors in [5] present an overview on the main problems and issues related to the development and maintenance of a LOR. Their work list the most commonly adopted software for the LOR and also describe their major characteristics. They also point out the usual problems a LOR faces, such as quality maintenance, long-term storage and integration with other LORs. These problems are also commented in [14].

In [19], the main objective of the authors was to conduct a study on how the current LORs could be used as a KMS (Knowledge Management System). The idea was to identify functionalities that could support the management of educational communities' explicit and tacit knowledge. The main result is a proposed a list of basic LOR functionalities that could improve the organization and sharing of information.

In [16], the authors present a quantitative analysis on the publication process of LOs. Their work found the statistical distributions that describe the nature of the publication process. Those results enables system architects to take better decision on how to improve the system architecture and infrastructure to support future demands.

In a work more related to this one, [17] presents an analysis of the LO metadata instances found at the GLOBE (Global Learning Objects Brokered Exchange) alliance. The authors present a detailed information profile on the use of the LOM attributes, such as the attributes most adopted by the creators, the average number of attributes that are completed filled, etc. This information can be useful for search systems and other related facilities.

The authors in [13] present the results of a comprehensive study on how the LORs are classified, their major features and usefulness. The results reported show the relevant role the LORs have on providing a trusted and knowledgeable source of quality educational information. Moreover, the authors list the basic functionalities present in most of the LORs, pointing out the ones that are more problematic, such as maintenance and updating.

This work is part of a larger effort, that differs from the previous ones as we intend not only to understand how the LOs are represented, but to propose a method to process and use them - regardless of their metadata standard - in search and recommender systems, such as the one proposed by [18]. This work describes the first steps towards our goal: we analyzed the size distribution of the LORs, their growth over time, and statistics about metadata completion and blank fields, and then discuss the implication of our findings on our future intents.

3 Learning Objects: Definitions and Standards

In this section, a number of previously proposed metadata standards for LOs are described, mainly the ones available in the LORs used to extract the metadata for our analysis.

3.1 IEEE-LOM

The IEEE-LOM [11] is an open standard for Leaning Object Metadata, published by the Institute of Electrical and Electronics Engineers Standards Association in 2002. Its main objective is to support the description of the several aspects of a LO and also their related vocabulary.

The IEEE LOM standard presents itself as a hierarchy of elements. The first layer comprises of nine categories and each one contains sub-elements. The sub-elements may be simple values or even an aggregation of other elements that can have sub-elements as well.

The way each element is used depends on context and semantics, which are defined in the LOM Data Model. For example, some elements such as *Description* and *Purpose* can appear only once within the same element container, others such as *Classification* can appear repeatedly.

Another relevant feature of the IEEE LOM standard regards the vocabulary (or domain values) of the simple elements. This is specified by the *value space* and *datatype* each simple data elements can hold. For example, some elements accept any Unicode string as input, but other elements have their input values already defined (i.e. controlled vocabulary) or must be in a specified format, such as dates.

3.2 Dublin Core

The Dublin Core Metadata Initiative - Education Metadata Set (DCMI-EMS), proposed by the DCMI in 2006 [7], presents an extended set of elements to describe educational resources.

Despite the fact that DCMI-EMS has an element set to describe educational resources, it does not have specific terms tailored to describe LOs. This is because DCMI-EMS is based on the 15 core elements of the original Dublin Core metadata set, and those elements are not as specific as the ones from IEEE-LOM for describing LOs. For that reason, some authors describe their LOs using DCMI-EMS elements in a similar way as existent IEEE-LOM fields.

Nonetheless, there has been relevant efforts on integrating DCMI-EMS and IEEE-LOM [8], aiming at solving technical differences between the standards. These differences are mainly related to the unification of the data models and acceptance of some IEEE-LOM fields on DCMI. In [1] the authors propose the reusability of metadata fields to ease the integration efforts between IEEE-LOM and DCMI-EMS.

3.3   OBAA

The OBAA metadata standard [20] was developed by the Federal University of Rio Grande do Sul (UFRGS) in partnership with the University of Vale dos Sinos (UNISINOS). The main idea the OBAA was the establishment of a standard specification for technical and functional requirements of a framework for producing, editing and distributing interactive digital content in the Web, mobile devices and digital television.

OBAA is based on the IEEE-LOM standard, it contains all the original categories and proposed the adoption of additional metadata, complementing the technical and educational categories and including two new categories representing accessibility and segmentation aspects.

The authors explain that using IEEE-LOM as the basis for OBAA would ease the reuse to the existence of a large amount of previously developed LOs in different standards. Another reason is the use of metadata profiles (reduced sets of metadata), directed to educational content developers. Through these profiles, they would make possible to meet different demands of specific niches of the educational community.

4   Learning Objects Repositories

In this section, we present and briefly comment the results of our analysis on the metadata we collected from several different learning object repositories (LORs) found in the Internet.

In our study, we were interested in retrieve metadata that was present in Learning Object Repositories that had the following characteristics: (1) allowed metadata retrieval by means of OAI-PMH connections (2) showed signs of still being in use, or, at least, not being completely unattended, such as date of last update and the state of their original website. After a throughout search, we retrieved the metadata from 19 international and 9 Brazilian repositories. The international LORs' metadata was divided into two sets: 11 were organized according to the Dublin Core ontology and 8 according to LOM. The Brazilian repositories were organized according to the Dublin Core standard, with the exception of Portal OBAA, which adopted OBAA. The size of the repositories is given by Table 1.

Combined, those 29 repositories have 905,878 LOs, with the international repositories containing 603,019 LOs (299,677 organized according to Dublin Core and 303,342 according to LOM) and the Brazilian repositories having 302,859 LOs.

For the remainder of this section, we will analyze separately the state of those three large groups of repositories: International Dublin Core (IDC), International LOM ($ILOM$) and Brazilian (BR). We aim not only to better understand their determining characteristics, but also to contrast the main differences in the creation of metadata in those large groups. Moreover, we are also specifically interested in verifying if the LOM repositories, which theoretically have more explicit metadata regarding the educational characteristics of the LOs they store, are indeed making full use of this feature.

Table 1. Number of learning objects in each of the repositories considered in this study, divided into (1) International Dublin Core repositories (2) Brazilian Dublin Core repositories (*except for 13, which is OBAA) (3) International LOM repositories. The IDs of the repositories are ordered by increasing size inside of each division

ID	Repository name	# of L.O.s
International Dublin Core repositories		
1	Athabasca University Library Institutional Repository (Auspace)	2180
2	LEKYTHOS	8524
3	Edinburgh Research Archive (ERA)	9140
4	Aberystwyth University Open Access Repository (Cadair)	13615
5	UNECA institutional repository	13778
6	University of Texas Digital Repository (UTDR)	14943
7	ResearchSpace@Auckland	22441
8	Oregon State University Libraries (OSU Libraries)	34732
9	Sistema de Información de la Facultad de Ciencias (UNAM)	43149
10	Scholarly Materials And Research @ Georgia Tech (SMARTech)	47332
11	DSpace@MIT	89843
Brazilian Dublin Core* repositories		
12	Repositório Digital OBAA	58
13	CESTA	596
14	Barcelona Digital Centro Tecnológico (BDigital)	3650
15	Biblioteca Digital da UFMG	12185
16	Banco Internacional de Objetos Educacionais	15669
17	Repositório Digital Institucional - UFPR	17414
18	Repositório Institucional da UFSC	51890
19	Acervo Digital da Unesp	96178
20	LUME Repositorio Digital	105219
International IEEE-LOM repositories		
21	Texas Learning Object Repository (TxLOR)	1334
22	Turkish Agricultural Learning Objects Repository	1530
23	Willkommen bei MELT - Metadata Ecology for Learning and Teaching	2251
24	Agricultural Learning Repository tool	2553
25	Natural Europe	6277
26	Canal-U	17047
27	Eurêka Le projet Eurêka	19578
28	Ariadne	252772

To better understand the size distributions of the repositories, we present in Fig. 1 the cumulative probability distribution over repository sizes. As can be seen, the IDC and BR repositories follow a similar behavior with most LOs present in the medium and large repositories. In contrast, most of the LOs found in ILOM repositories were from ARIADNE [15], which is an aggregator of LOs from a number of different LORs, while all other repositories are significantly smaller than it, with sizes in the medium size range in comparison with the ones present in IDC and BR repositories.

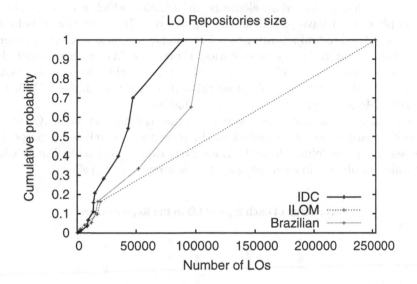

Fig. 1. Cumulative distribution over repository sizes

Regarding the nature of the LOs studied, we were also interested in verifying exactly which are the types of LO stored in those repositories. We divided the LOs in 4 categories: Documents, comprised of objects with the pdf, xls, doc and similar extensions; Images, comprised of image types such as png, tiff, jpeg and others; Multimedia, with video and audio related extensions such as mp4, mpeg, wav, real audio; and Others, containing objects like java class files, zip compressed files, octet-stream and others. The number of objects found of each category is shown in Table 2.

The vast majority of the LOs found is comprised of documents. This means that text related documents still are the preferred educational media for LO

Table 2. Number of LOs per type

Type	Number of LOs
Images	25,827
Documents	344,717
Multimedia	55,364
Other	8,309

creators. However, we also verified the noticeable amount of multimedia LOs, of more than 10 % of number of text LOs.

It is important to notice the total the number of objects in those categories, 434,217, is much smaller than the total number of objects present in the repositories, 905,878. This occurred because we have determined the type of the Learning Object by its format metadata elements, information which a large number of LOs simply did not have present in the repositories. To circumvent this limitation, we also tried to find repositories where the type element gave clear description of the format (in many repositories, there were LOs with typemetadata descriptions such as "Article", "Image", "Recording", which were then assigned to their respective categories). Without this extra step, the number of LOs with the format Metadata present was less than 350,000.

As we analyzed the data, we also realized that the proportion of LOs in each category is vastly different depending on the repository, as well as the proportion of elements with undefined format. These facts can be noticed in Fig. 2, where the number of objects in each category for each repository is shown.

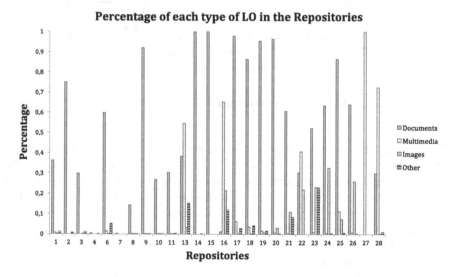

Fig. 2. LOs category type distribution

As can be seen, the vast majority of the Dublin Core repositories (both International and Brazilian) are comprised of documents (mostly pdf files), with two Brazilian repositories being responsible for most of the multimedia and image LOs found in Dublin Core LORs (13 and 16). Also it is important to show that a significant number of repositories do not have format information for all their LOs, which could have negative repercussion in the performance of more advanced information retrieval and recommendation algorithms, that could use this information to present LOs more adequate to the learning needs and profile of students. Moreover, two of the repositories, (5 and 12) did not have any easily accessible information about the format of its LOs.

On the other hand, the format description of LOs in LOM repositories were substantially more complete, with all repositories having more than 90 % of their LOs with format information present, with the exception of 21, that still had 80 % of its LOs format described. This might strongly suggest that LOM repositories might be more well described in regards with its metadata in comparison with Dublin Core ones.

4.1 Repositories Growth Analysis

Another important question we intended to answer in our research was regarding the number of LOs that are added to the repositories over the time. Data related to the number of new LOs that were stored in the LORs over time was collected for all 29 repositories. To simplify our analysis on the data, the repositories were divided in 3 size classes: small (up to 10,000 LOs), medium (from 10,000 and up to a little more than 20,0000 LOs) and larger (above 30,0000 LOs). The repositories were also divided between International Dublin Core, International LOM and Brazilian for english and portuguese content, respectively. The results are presented in Fig. 3.

Results show the consistent increasing number of LOs being created and stored over time in all repositories, regardless of their language and size. The only repository for which we can not present this information is repository number 26 (MELT), since it did not have any kind of date of publication metadata present for its LOs. Moreover, repositories 24, 25 and 27, which also use LOM metadata, do not have date of publication metadata present for all their LOs, thus leading to their curves not reaching 100 %. This result might indicate that for some LOM repository users, updating the date of creation is not essential when inserting a new LO in their repositories.

Overall, it can be seen that repositories do present different growth characteristics: it is noticeable that new LOs are being stored in a flood pattern (straight up lines) in some repositories, as well as in a flow pattern (slow ascendant lines) in others. Another aspect that these results show is that there is no direct correlation between the age of the LOR and its number of LOs, since we have, for instance, repository 10 (UNAM), which is 40 months old, and repository 20 (Acervo Digital da Unesp), that is only 17 months old, which are both bigger than most of the studied repositories, with both also presenting a visible growth surge. A somewhat similar behavior is also seem in our largest repository, ARIADNE, in which in the first 110 months had a relatively small number of LOs being added constantly, only for, in the spam of 8 months have a large addition of LOs in a visible flood pattern. This behavior indicates that probably at some moment there was a concentrated effort to add a large number of LOs to those repositories.

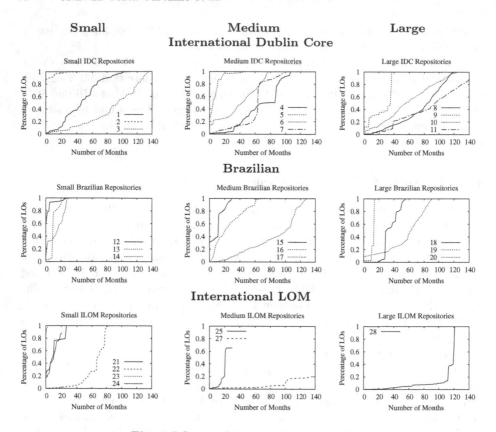

Fig. 3. LO growth in repositories over time

4.2   Metadata Completion Analysis

One critical aspect regarding the potential reuse of LOs is the completion of their metadata. The larger the number and more complete descriptions are available at the metadata fields, the more useful the LO can be. In Fig. 4, we present the maximum, minimum and average number of elements found in the metadata of the LOs for each repository we collected.

As can be noticed, the average number of metadata entries found in LOs can be considered small, with an overall average of 30 metadata entries per LO. Other behavior observed is some of the repositories it that there is a very large variation in the number of metadata that an LO present in it might have. One desirable feature of a LOR is a consistency on how its metadata is filled for its LOs, since this metadata is one of the best ways to access and understand the LOs present in the dataset. Using repositories with a big difference between its minimum and maximum number of metadata for LOs and, more importantly, repositories with a large variation in the metadata fulfillment values (shown by the standard deviation error bars in Fig. 4 might lead to wild variations in the perception of the state of the LOs of this repository.

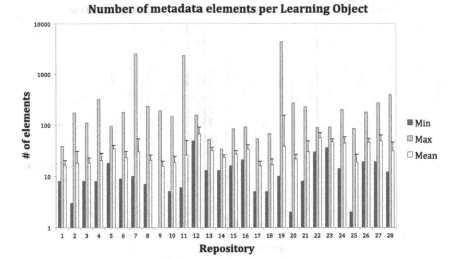

Fig. 4. Number of metadata elements in LOs per repository

In Fig. 4, it can be easily seen that many repositories have a very stable metadata creation criteria, seen as a smaller variation in the number of metadata entries present, such as 1, 3, 5, 6, 8, 9, 10, 11, 13, 14, 15, 16, 17, 20 and all LOMs with the exception of 21 and 28. Conversely, repositories such as 2, 7, 11, and especially 19 had a very large standard deviation, which might indicate a lack of consistency in its LO metadata creation, which could potentially pose a number of hardships for data normalization, deduplication and many other algorithms that would use this data.

To better highlight how inconstant is the metadata completion when comparing different repositories, we also present information about the completion of the most common and significative element fields of the Dublin Core, OBAA and LOM repositories. Figure 5 shows the metadata completion levels for relevant element fields for Dublin Core repositories, such as *Subject*, *Description* and *Format*.

As can be seen, with the exception of the title, even those essential fields were not filled in many of the Dublin Core repositories. In some repositories, LOs were found with only the *Title* field complete. Moreover, only repository 14 had their Title, Subject and Description fields filled for all its LOs consistently, with all other repositories lacking one or more of those. This scenario poses significant challengers for the LOs retrieval and reusability, because of these scarce and fragmented metadata.

For the LOM repositories, besides the basic fields such as *Title*, *Description* and *Format*, it is also important to verify the level of completion of the metadata fields related to educational characteristics of the learning objects. The fields we chose to verify were *Keywords*, *Coverage*, *Context*, *Learning Resource Type*, *Interactivity Type and Level*, *Semantic Density*, *Intended End User Role*,

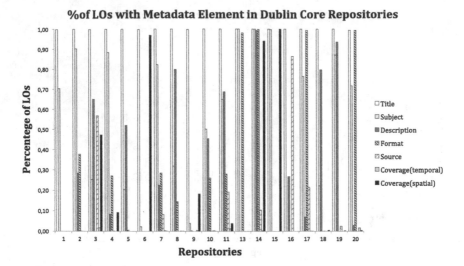

Fig. 5. Completion of important element fields in Dublin Core LORs.

Typical Age Range and *Difficulty* (*Typical Learning Time* is not shown since only repository 23 had any significant amount of LOs with it). Figure 6 presents the completion rate for those metadata fields for each LOM repository. We also present the results for repository 12, which has the OBAA format, that has all of those fields in common with LOM repositories.

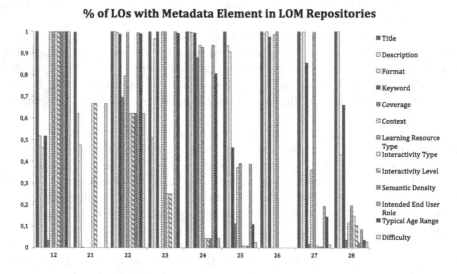

Fig. 6. Completion of important element fields in LOM LORs.

For the more general fields such as *Title*, *Description* and *Format*, it can be seen that the LOM repositories usually show much more regularity, with most of them consistently presenting high levels of completion, having the *Title* field being basically present in all LOs of all repositories, while the others usually being present in at least 50 % or more of the LOs. This is an indication that those repositories might be more generally well kept in comparison with Dublin Core ones.

However, regarding to the more education-centric fields, which should theoretically be the main advantage of LOM in comparison to Dublin Core, the completion levels are much less consistent. Repositories 12 and 22 were the ones with the higher levels of metadata completion, with almost all metadata with completion levels of at least 50 %. However, both those repositories are among the smaller collected, and this reduced size probably leading to a more careful manual curation of their LOs metadata.

As the size of the repositories increase (i.e. larger repository ID), the proportion of completion of education-related metadata is greatly reduced, with *intended end-user role* being one of the most used in the larger repositories (with the exception of 26). One interesting case to consider is the case of ARIADNE(28), the largest LOM repository considered in this work. While the education metadata completion ratio is relatively on the low side (lower than 20 %), when considering its size (around 25,000 LOs), this would mean around 2000–4000 LOs more consistently annotated.

Table 3. Total number of LOs in our dataset containing each metadata field studied in this work.

General metadata		
Name	Absolute total	% of LOs
Title	905132	99.92 %
Description	581229	64.16 %
Format	264463	29.2 %
Keyword	225443	24.89 %
Coverage	64919	7.17 %
LOM specific metadata		
Name	Absolute total	% of LOM LOs
Learning resource type	94868	31.43 %
Interactivity type	40282	13.34 %
Interactivity level	29200	9.67 %
Semantic density	7504	2.48 %
Intended end user role	33872	11.22 %
Typical age range	18416	6.10 %
Difficulty	9375	3.10 %

In order to have a better overview of the state of the metadata on the LOs present in the repositores considered in this work, in Table 3 we present the overall number of LOs containing each metadata field that was considered in this work.

As can be seen, the *Title* is the only metadata element that can be considered to be consistently present in all LOs, while *Description* is the only other besides *Title* that is present in more than 40 % of the LOs. When considering metadata fields that pertain specifically to LOM LORs, the completion levels are even lower. Aside from the *Resource Type*, no other of the considered metadata was present in more than 14 % of the LOs. Thus, we believe that researchers considering using information about LOs in an automatic fashion, should take this rate of completion in consideration when estimating the number of Learning Objects that can be fully utilized.

5   Conclusions and Future Work

Learning object repositories (LOs) have been supporting the increasing widespread of web-based learning environments. Using them, teachers and students can interact remotely at any time and from different physical locations, sharing activities and content that is based on the massive use of LOs.

However, there are huge amounts of LOs available in the Internet and they are store in several different LO Repositories (LORs), being described in different metadata standards. Thus, the same LO can be found in several different repositories and with different descriptions. In addition, a relevant number of them have incomplete descriptions or no description at all. This situation creates a problem for services such as search and recommendation.

This work presents the results of a quantitative analysis of a number of international and Brazilian LORs, with a focus on how the contributors organize their metadata, the frequency of updates in the repository and overall characteristics of the Learning Objects present. A total of 29 LORs were accessed and the metadata related to 905,878 LOs was collected.

An analysis was conducted on the size distribution of the LORs, their growth over time, and statistics about metadata completion. We verified that while many repositories have a large number of LOs, their organization might vary largely. We verified that a small number of very large LORs contained most of the LOs found, and that while a very large number of LOs were textual documents, there was a significant number of multimedia LOs, coming mainly from 2 repositories.

Regarding metadata completion, we showed that, overall most repositories have relatively poor metadata for its stored LOs. This is a strong indicator that, in order to harness the full potential of this metadata, more work has to be done in order to either manually add this metadata or to try to generate it in an automated fashion. We believe that this is an important future work to be done to lead to an improved use of this information.

As a more immediate future work, we intend to go further in our task of building a search and recommending system for LOs. Our next steps are to clean and standardize some LO attributes (such as contributors names and descriptions) and deduplicate and perform record linkage in all the LO records in the repositories that we have collected, leading to a unified repository containing all their LOs.

References

1. Abdul Karim, A.H., Chaudhry, A.S., Khoo, C.S.: Learning objects application profile for granularity and reusability: integrating dublin core with IEEE-LOM. In: Proceedings of the 2007 International Conference on Dublin Core and Metadata Applications: Application Profiles: Theory and Practice, pp. 116–122. Dublin Core Metadata Initiative (2007)
2. Bell, R., Dravis, F.: Is you data dirty? and does that matter? accenture Whiter Paper (2006). http://www.accenture.com
3. Carini, R.M., Kuh, G.D., Klein, S.P.: Student engagement and student learning: testing the linkages*. Res. High. Educ. **47**(1), 1–32 (2006)
4. de Carvalho, M.G., Laender, A.H.F., Gonçalves, M.A., da Silva, A.S.: A genetic programming approach to record deduplication. IEEE Trans. Knowl. Data Eng. **24**(3), 399–412 (2012). http://doi.ieeecomputersociety.org/10.1109/TKDE.2010.234
5. Cervone, H.F.: Digital learning object repositories. OCLC Syst. Serv. Int. Digital Libr. Perspect. **28**(1), 14–16 (2012)
6. Dede, C., Richards, J.: Digital Teaching Platforms: Customizing Classroom Learning for Each Student. Teachers College Press, New York (2012)
7. Dekkers, M., Weibel, S.: State of the dublin core metadata initiative, April 2003. D-Lib Mag. **9**(4), 1082–9873 (2003)
8. Hodgins, W., Weibel, S.: Memorandum of understanding between the dublin core metadata initiative and the IEEE learning technology standards committee (2000)
9. Koster, A., Primo, T.T., Koch, F.L., Oliveira, A., Chung, H.: Towards a educator-centred digital teaching platform: the ground conditions for a data-driven approach. In: Proceedings of the 15th IEEE International Conference on Advanced Learning Technologies (ICALT 2015) (2015)
10. Lehman, R.: Learning object repositories. New Dir. Adult Continuing Educ. **2007**(113), 57–66 (2007)
11. McClelland, M.: Metadata standards for educational resources. Computer **36**(11), 107–109 (2003)
12. McGreal, R.: Online Education Using Learning Objects. Psychology Press, London (2004)
13. McGreal, R.: A typology of learning object repositories. In: Adelsberger, H.H., Kinshuk, Pawlowski, J.M., Sampson, D.G. (eds.) Handbook on Information Technologies for Education and Training, pp. 5–28. Springer, Heidelberg (2008)
14. Mohan, P.: Learning object repositories. In: Informing Science and IT Education Joint Conference (2005)
15. Najjar, J., Duval, E., Ternier, S., Neven, F.: Towards interoperable learning object repositories: the ariadne experience. In: ICWI, pp. 219–226 (2003)
16. Ochoa, X., Duval, E.: Quantitative analysis of learning object repositories. IEEE Trans. Learn. Technol. **2**(3), 226–238 (2009)
17. Ochoa, X., Klerkx, J., Vandeputte, B., Duval, E.: On the use of learning object metadata: the GLOBE experience. In: Kloos, C.D., Gillet, D., Crespo García, R.M., Wild, F., Wolpers, M. (eds.) EC-TEL 2011. LNCS, vol. 6964, pp. 271–284. Springer, Heidelberg (2011)

18. Primo, T.T., Vicari, R.M.: A recommender system that allows reasoning and interoperability over educational content metadata. In: 2011 11th IEEE International Conference on Advanced Learning Technologies (ICALT), pp. 598–599. IEEE (2011)
19. Sampson, D.G., Zervas, P.: Learning object repositories as knowledge management systems. Knowl. Manage. E-Learn. Int. J. (KM&EL) 5(2), 117–136 (2013)
20. Viccari, R., Gluz, J., Passerino, L., Santos, E., Primo, T., Rossi, L., Roesler, V.: The OBAA proposal for learning objects supported by agents. In: Proceedings of MASEIE Workshop-AAMAS (2010)
21. Wheatley, M.: Operation clean data. CIO Asia Magazine, August 2004. http://www.cio-asia.com
22. Wiley, D.A.: Instructional use of learning objects. Agency for Instructional Technology (2001)

Towards an Intelligent Learning Objects Based Model for Dynamic E-Learning Content Selection

João de Amorim Jr.[(⊠)] and Ricardo Azambuja Silveira

PPGCC – UFSC, Florianópolis, Brazil
joao.amorim.jr@gmail.com, ricardo.silveira@ufsc.br

Abstract. This paper presents a model for selecting Learning Objects (LO) for e-learning based on the multi-agent paradigm and aiming to facilitate the use of LOs in an adaptive way in Virtual Learning Environments. The proposed framework extends the Intelligent Learning Objects approach through the use of a BDI agent architecture, allowing the communication with the instructional resources that constitute the LO according to the SCORM standard. The agents' reasoning process uses the elements obtained during the interaction between the student and the object, enabling the building of enhanced dynamic learning experiences. The LMS Moodle was used to validate this proposed model. A prototype and their integration with the LMS Moodle were developed to evaluate the computational feasibility of the proposed model. At last, course simulations were performed, resulting in improved learning experiences.

Keywords: Dynamic learning experience · LO · LMS · BDI · Multi-agent system

1 Introduction

Distance learning plays an important role in the educational process worldwide. Many learning institutions have adopted e-learning as one of their active strategies and new approaches to on-line education are becoming more and more common [1].

Teaching-aid systems must be geared to enhancing the educational experience. Two aspects contribute to this: adaptability and re-use. The former is related to different students' needs and styles. An adaptable system increases the student understanding in a personalized way [2–4]. The latter avoids the cost of developing a new resource if one already exists with the same learning objectives [3, 5].

Intelligent Tutoring Systems (ITS), Learning Management Systems (LMS) and Learning Objects (LO) are some computational tools that enrich the learning process. ITSs are applications created for a specific educational domain, usually including adaptability and interoperability resources [6]. LMSs are learning environments used to build on-line courses (or to publish material) to monitor student progress and to manage educational data [1, 7, 8]. Finally, LOs are digital artifacts for supporting the teaching-learning process, promoting reuse and adaptability [9].

© Springer International Publishing Switzerland 2016
F. Koch et al. (Eds.): SOCIALEDU 2015, CCIS 606, pp. 65–82, 2016.
DOI: 10.1007/978-3-319-39672-9_6

Although LOs and LMSs allow reusability, they have a limited level of adaptability. The kind of adaptation they offer needs to be pre-programmed by the instructional designer or teacher, that is, this systems usually are not dynamically adaptable [10, 11].

This article presents the first results of our research that seeks the convergence of these three different paradigms for the development of intelligent learning environments. Our proposed multi-agent model uses data from the LMS, from the LO metadata and, most importantly, from the interaction between the student and the LO while it is occurring. Based on this set of information the agents can decide whether the student needs to interact with a new LO and where this is the case, which LO it should be.

The first step of the design method used in our research was to identify related works and in particular any issues that could be improved and extended. The second step was to design the Multi-Agent System (MAS) following an Agent-Oriented Software Engineering (AOSE) methodology [12]. The third step was to develop the MAS, which is composed of a search engine and delivery and presentation systems, to retrieve learning objects from repositories. This structure was implemented on the Jadex platform [13, 14].

We were then able to integrate the proposed MAS with the SCORM learning object standard technology [15, 16]. The SCORM is a model of interoperable LO, adopted in online education worldwide, and compatible with most LMSs. The SCORM API provides data from the student interaction with the LO in real time. Therefore the agents can use the interaction data to deliberate and act. We also developed a plug-in that allows access to the features of the proposed MAS within a LMS Moodle course. Finally we evaluated the computational feasibility of our proposed model in course simulations. In the next section we review the related work found identified in the first step.

2   Related Work

There have been several similar studies which have developed approaches to providing adaptability to educational systems. Some of them are built as an extension of an LMS using conditional jumps [10], Bayesian networks [4] or data mining techniques [7] as their adaptive strategy. Other approaches are not integrated with a LMS but use distinct ways to adapt the learning to the students' style. Examples include ITS [8] and the Recommender system [2, 17, 18].

Other approaches have been developed based on the multi-agent system (MAS) approach. MASs are composed of autonomous entities (agents) which perceive the environment they are situated in and act on it to achieve their objectives. The communication and cooperation of individual agents make it possible to solve complex problems which they could not solve individually [19–21].

An important MAS architecture for intelligent agents is the BDI model. BDI agents are composed of mental attitudes (belief, desire, intention) and act following the practical reasoning process (goal deliberation and means-end reasoning) [20, 22]. Some analyzed works combine MAS and MOODLE [23] to make the LMS more adaptive. An example is the use of information obtained from the forum to show resources and other activities to the students [24]. There is also an adaptive environment based on agents that are able to identify the student cognitive profile [25].

However all of these related studies have two characteristics that can be improved. The first is the way a student's learning style is identified. The studies analyzed used questionnaires at the beginning of the course to do this. This step can be considered intrusive and distracting [2]. Some studies avoid this by clustering the students in profiles based on their assessments grades [25].

The second area for improvement is the possibility of dynamically coupling new learning resources (LO) to the environment. The teacher or instructional designer needs to configure in advance all of the possible course paths for each student style. This is difficult and time consuming [4, 26]. If a new LO needs to be attached to the course then the teacher/instructional designer must modify the course structure.

Based on this review of related work we observed that the main points arising were: what information were used on the definition of the student model; which were the supported learning object standards; how to access data arising from the interaction of student with the environment; how to integrate with LMS; and what kind of adaptability is achieved. Table 1 shows the comparison between this work and related researches.

Table 1. Comparison of the related work and the proposed model

Paper	Student model	LO standards	Check interaction	LMS	Adaptive context
Moura and Fernandes [27]	Survey	No	No	No	LMS
Vesin et al. [2]	Survey	SCORM	No	No	LMS
Carvalho et al. [28]	Survey	LOM	No	No	LMS
Bachari et al. [4]	Survey	LOM	No	Yes	LMS
Despotovic et al. [7]	Survey	No	No	Yes	LMS
Alencar and Netto [24]	Forum	No	No	Yes	LMS
Giuffra and Silveira [25]	Appraisal	No	No	Yes	LMS
Bremgartner et al. [29]	Survey, appraisal and frequency	No	No	Yes	LMS
Pereira et al. [30]	Facebook	LOM	No	No	LMS
Frade et al. [31]	Context	SCORM	No	No	LMS
Santos et al. [32]	Interaction	SCORM (extended)	Yes	No	LMS
This research	Appraisal and interaction	LOM and SCORM	Yes	Yes	Object

Based on the characteristics highlighted in Table 1, we have designed a model that should enhance learning experiences performed in LMS courses, and based on objects which are in conformance with learning resources standards (IEEE-LOM [11] metadata and SCORM model). The solution uses data from the interaction with the student to decide dynamically what LO will be presented, so that the adaptive context is the LO itself.

The next section presents more details about the proposed model.

3 Proposed Model

The proposed model is based on a MAS approach integrated with an LMS. This builds on the related works analyzed by allowing an LO to be included dynamically in the learning experience, adding intelligent behavior to the system.

The adaptability of the solution is based on the possibility of a new LO being attached to the LMS, without advance course configuration, but as soon as the system identifies that the student needs to reinforce their understanding on a specific concept. This can be automatically identified through the verification of the student performance (grade) on each instructional unit, or by student choice when interacting with the LO. Moreover, the course structure becomes more flexible, since it is not necessary to configure all of the possible sets of learning paths for each student profile.

The proposed model achieves re-use by the combination of pre-existing and validated LOs whose topic matches the topic that the student needs to learn more about. This avoids the need for teachers or instructional designers need to build new materials.

To produce more intelligent LOs, previous works proposed the convergence between the LO and MAS technologies, called Intelligent Learning Objects (ILO) [15, 33]. This approach makes it possible to offer more adaptive, reusable and complete learning experiences. An ILO is an agent capable of playing the role of a LO, which can acquire new knowledge by the interaction with students and other ILOs (agents information exchange), raising the potential of student's understanding.

The LO metadata permits the identification of the educational topic related to the LO [11]. Hence the ILOs (agents) are able to identify what subject is associated with the learning experience shown to the student and then to show complementary information (another ILO) to address the student's lack of knowledge in that area of the subject.

The objective of this research is to improve the framework developed to build ILOs based on MAS with BDI (belief, desire, intention) architecture [34], extending the model to allow the production of adaptive and reusable learning experiences. The idea is to dynamically select ILOs in the LMS, without previous specific configuration on the course structure, according to the information obtained during the learning session, such as the student performance.

The new model, which we have named Intelligent Learning Object Multi-Agent System (ILOMAS), is composed of agents with specific goals, capable of communicating and offering learning resources to students in an LMS course. The agents can monitor the interaction between the student and the learning object, and obtain information about this interaction through the SCORM API.

The ILOMAS model is detailed in the next few sections of this paper. Its design, implementation and validation processes are described in the context of the features of the tools, platforms and technologies employed on the ILOMAS development.

The next section deepens the analysis and design of the agent model, which constitutes the most important part of the ILOMAS.

4 Analysis and Design

The modeling of the ILOMAS framework was done using an agent-oriented software engineering methodology. The Prometheus methodology defines a detailed process to specify, design and implement intelligent agent systems based on goals, plans and beliefs (BDI architecture) [35]. This is composed of several activities and phases which generate specification and design documents. Another reason to choose this methodology was the existence of the Prometheus Design Tool (PDT), an Eclipse IDE plug-in which supplies an iterative design of the Prometheus diagrams [12].

During the system specification phase of Prometheus, the goals, roles, agents and their respective interfaces with the environment (perceptions, actions and external data) were identified. As result, two kinds of agents were detected (Fig. 1):

- LMSAgent – This represents the LMS. It is responsible for (1) receiving the student learning experience request (*Learning Experience Request* perception); (2) identifying the student grade (in the course) and the subject that the student must learn about (*Learning Experience Subject Identifier* role), according to the information provided from the LMS database (external data); and (3) for passing the control of the interaction with the student to a new agent of the kind ILOAgent (*Inform Learning Object Subject* message).
- ILOAgent – This is the agent responsible for showing the learning experience to the student. This is made through the presentation of an LO related to the subject that the student needs to learn about (the course's current topic), as identified by the LMSAgent. The function of an ILOAgent is to search a corresponding learning object on the LO repository (*Learning Object Searcher* role), based on the elements of the object metadata (in accordance with IEEE-LOM standard). In addition, the ILOAgent shows the selected LO to the student (*Learning Experience Show* action). This kind of agent must keep itself aware of the interaction between the student and the system (*Learning Object Player* role). This means that the ILOAgent gets data from this interaction i.e. the elements of SCORM data model such as session time, grade and progress measure. This set of data is used by the ILOAgent's *deliberation mechanism*, which defines whether the student needs a complementary learning experience. If so, an extra LO will be displayed (i.e.: due to access lateness). Otherwise, the student keeps interacting with the current LO.

The Agent overview diagram (Fig. 2) presents the agent's plans (the concrete way to achieve the agent's goals [20]), perceptions, actions, internal messages and capabilities. The idea of using capabilities is to put agent features into modules, allowing the re-use of commons characteristics (plans and goals) among distinct agents [35].

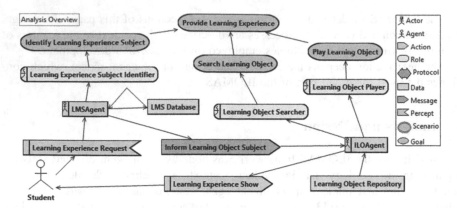

Fig. 1. Analysis overview

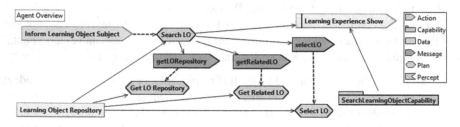

Fig. 2. Agent overview diagram (ILOAgent)

The next section presents details of the ILOMAS model implementation.

5   Implementation

Following the modeling phase the ILOMAS framework was implemented and a prototype developed to validate the proposed model. The Jadex framework [13, 14] (an extension of the JADE platform enhanced to develop intelligent agent systems) was chosen to implement the agents based on the BDI architecture [20, 22].

The Jadex platform permits the creation of active components, an approach that benefits from the association of two distinct technologies — Agents and SCA. The SCA model was proposed by the major IT companies (IBM, ORACLE) with the intention of promoting interoperability among distributed applications, according to concepts of components and service oriented architecture (SOA) [13, 14].

The newest Jadex platform version is Jadex BDI V3. Before V3 the agents were built in ADF files (XML tags for beliefs, desires, etc.) and Java classes (plans) [36]. However, in V3 the agents are developed using only pure Java classes (without XML files) and the annotations mechanism [14, 22]. What is more, in V3 the recommended method of agent communication is through service invocation. The BDI agents can be service providers (declaring specific annotations and implementing specific interfaces) and can request services from other agents, components, etc. [13, 14].

It is important to point out the implementation limitations. Instead of placing the emphasis on visualization issues (such as formats, rich graphical user interfaces, etc.), the MAS development was emphasized (with the agents and their interactions).

The interaction interface between the student and the agents' environment was implemented based on Java Servlets and JSP technologies, benefitting from the Jadex BDI V3 services communication structure. The Servlets technology allows the execution of services and Java classes at the server side of Web requests.

On the prototype, the servlet tier delegates the handling of the student browser request to a Java class (non-agent) based on the Facade design pattern. This pattern provides a unified and simplified interface to a sub-system, promoting low coupling [37]. The ILOMASFacade class offers access to agents' services (the agents' capabilities, plans, etc.) to the servlet classes, keeping the separation between the MAS tier and the external items (front-end and servlets), and avoiding unnecessary coupling (Fig. 3).

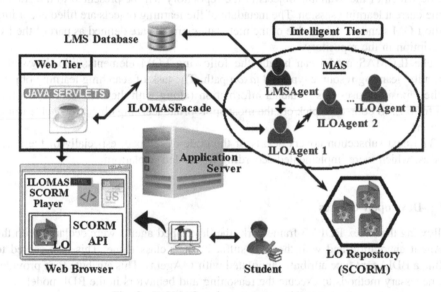

Fig. 3. ILOMAS web prototype architecture

The ILOMAS architecture also facilitates the integration with SCORM API and SCORM Run-Time Environment (RTE) [16] which are based on web technologies such as JavaScript and HTML. Thus the elements of the SCORM data model, which are obtained from the learning session (the period of interaction between the student and the LO), can be easily sent to the ILOMAS intelligent tier (the agents' environment), through a customized SCORM player. The strategy of sending data to and receiving data from a server asynchronously (AJAX [38]) enabled the Web tier (SCORM player) to send the SCORM elements to the ILOMAS and receive decisions about the learning flow made by the ILO Agent.

The integration with the SCORM API admits that the ILOMAS uses the data model elements to define the student's knowledge level, and to evaluate the status of the current experience (learning session). Some available elements are the learner's answers to quizzes (result), the elapsed time since the beginning of the interaction (latency), the weighting of the interaction status relative to others and a description of the LO's objectives [16]. If the learner displays difficulty in some subject (e.g. giving several incorrect answers in a row on the SCORM quiz, or taking a long time to interact with the LO without any progress), it is possible to make decisions based on the historical received data.

Therefore, the data received from the SCORM RTE were defined as the ILO Agent's beliefs. The ILO Agent's reasoning process uses its beliefs to determine whether: (1) a new complementary LO must be shown, according to the metadata of the related object; or (2) the student will continue interacting with the current LO. If so, the ILO Agent will keep monitoring the interaction with this current LO (re-starting the reasoning cycle [22].

Furthermore, as mentioned before, the ILO Agent also uses the LO metadata to decide which of the available objects in the repository will be presented to the student in the current learning session. The metadata of the learning objects are filled according to the LOM standard. The value of the metadata elements are defined as part of the LO description in the repository.

The ILOMAS model can handle the following LOM elements: title, keywords, difficulty, learning resource type and *taxon* path. The task of searching learning objects in the repository uses this metadata information (along with the data from interaction and from LMS course) to pick out the most appropriate learning object for that learning session.

The next subsection covers details of the code developed, especially of the agent classes, which were implemented according to the Jadex platform.

5.1 Developed Classes

Following the Jadex BDI V3 framework, the developed agents were declared with the @Agent annotation and with the BDI suffix in their class name. This also served to define a BDIAgent type attribute (annotated with @Agent). This attribute type provides the necessary methods to execute the reasoning and behaviors in the BDI model, such as dispatch an agent goal (leading to plan execution).

Other annotations can be used in BDI agent classes to declare attributes (@Belief, @Capability, etc.) as well as methods. The method annotations define agent behavior at specific states of the agent's life cycle such as @AgentCreated (after agent start up), @AgentKilled (before agent dies) and @AgentBody (agent runs) [14, 22, 39], When the ILOAgentBDI starts running its goal of searching what LO will be shown to the student is dispatched according to the subject identified by the LMSAgentBDI. The agents were defined as service providers using the annotations @Service and @ProvidedService, and implementing the methods of the Java Interface corresponding to each respective service, whose return is asynchronous [14, 39].

The BDI elements (beliefs, goals and plans) related to the functionality of identifying the subject associated with the learning experience were grouped in the IdentifyLearningExperienceCapability class. Another class developed was SearchLearning ObjectCapability which is composed of the sub-goals (1) identify the repository, (2) get the list of LOs associated with the subject within the repository, and (3) choose one LO. Some metadata elements defined in IEEE-LOM [11] are used in this process. The ILOAgentBDI has the SearchLearningObjectCapability which uses the elements "keywords" and "difficulty" of the LOM metadata to define the list of related LOs.

It is important to explain that the ILOAgent deliberation process follows the Jadex BDI mechanism, which is an extension of the PRS architecture [22]. So the agent class and methods are coded using the annotations (and their parameters) and classes of the Jadex framework related to goal creation conditions (@GoalCreationCondition), goal maintain condition (@GoalMaintainCondition), goal deliberation, conflicts and priorities (@Deliberation, @GoalInhibit) and plan triggers (@Plan, @Trigger).

As an example it is useful to highlight one of the goal prioritization strategies that was implemented. The goal related to present a new (extra) LO has higher priority than the goal of keeping the display of the current LO. Thus, the Jadex engine selects the goal related to show an extra LO instead of the goal of keeping the current LO, when both goals are valid to be pursued.

The next section presents the evaluations and experiments performed to validate and check the computational feasibility of the ILOMAS model.

6   Evaluation

The process of evaluating ILOMAS was made in two phases. The first phase was the validation of the prototype. The second phase involved the validation of the new ILOMAS version, which is SCORM compliant and has integration with the LMS Moodle. It is important to say that the focus of the evaluation was the computational feasibility and not the educational effectiveness.

These evaluations phases are detailed in the upcoming subsections.

6.1   First ILOMAS Validation

The first prototype was deployed on an Apache Tomcat server (7.0.57) hosted in an Ubuntu system (14.04.1) to test the proposed model. At the beginning of the test a student accessed the system and the LMSAgent identified that the student needed to learn about photosynthesis (biology course). The student request for the learning experience lead to a new servlet request. This servlet has forwarded the student request to ILOMASFacade class, which waited for the end of ILOAgentBDI's deliberation. The agent identified an LO within the repository related to the subject. Finally, this LO was shown to the student successfully.

A student request (by pressing the corresponding button) for a complementary learning experience was also simulated. As result, a new ILOAgentBDI was created on the system, which searched for and found a different LO related to the same subject (photosynthesis) within the repository.

It was not explicitly defined in the database that the student should have watched this new LO (only the subject was required, but no specific LO), so the MAS obtained the related LO dynamically (Fig. 4).

Fig. 4. ILOMAS web prototype

The next subsection presents the Moodle extension (plug-in) developed to allow the integration of ILOMAS features in LMS Moodle.

6.2   ILOIR: Moodle Plug-in

The next step in evaluating the proposed model was the seamless integration of the ILOMAS environment and the LMS Moodle so that the student does not need to leave the virtual environment to access another system resulting in possible loss of attention. To achieve this we developed a plug-in for the LMS as an interface resource to the smart learning objects. We called this ILOIR (Intelligent Learning Object's Resource interface). This feature allows the teacher to define the subject (theme) and learning objective for that instructional unit as well as the address where the ILOMAS platform is available (Fig. 5).

Fig. 5. Configuration of the ILOIR resource added to an introductory course of Brazilian Social Security Law in Moodle (created in Portuguese).

Furthermore, the ILOIR plug-in provides the functionality of the ILOMAS system for the student, within Moodle. The developed extension engages the ILOMAS' web tier (SCORM player, container HTML and JavaScript library) with the LMS structure, allowing the features within Moodle to establish communication (indirect) with the agents of the environment.

The next subsection describes the experiments performed to evaluate the computational feasibility of the ILOMAS model.

6.3 Experiments

Experiments were carried out to evaluate the computational feasibility of the proposed model. Therefore an introductory course in Brazilian Social Security Law offered by the school of a statewide government public agency (from Brazil) was created based on the ILOMAS architecture.

We aimed to evaluate two types of scenario: one of course settings and the other of student interaction with the new ILOIR feature. To this end we performed comparisons between two Portuguese language courses created in Moodle.

The first course (Course 1, Fig. 6) had three learning objects related to Brazilian Social Security Law (available in the repository) added directly as resources of the SCORM type (native in Moodle). The second course (Course 2, Fig. 7) was set with only one resource of the ILOIR type (the new plug-in developed) whose subject refers to the subject of the first SCORM object inserted in Course 1.

Fig. 6. Structure of the course with the SCORM resources – Course 1.

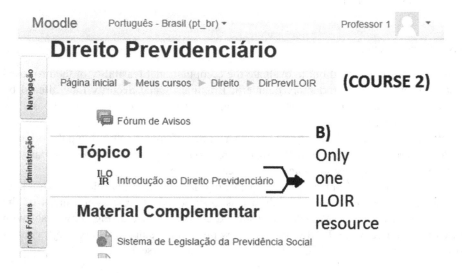

Fig. 7. Structure of the course with the ILOIR resource – Course 2.

Table 2 compares the two Moodle courses. The use of the ILOIR feature reduces the number items to be added to the course structure, resulting in a smaller setup time. However the main benefit is in the number of objects that may be used in the learning session (experience) by the student. The course that uses the explicitly included LOs has only these objects available. On the other hand the course using the plug-in ILOIR (which supports the Intelligent Learning Objects from ILOMAS environment) allows the presentation of several different LOs to the student, dynamically, during the experiment, provided these objects are related to the topic set by the teacher in ILOIR feature. This feature offered by the plug-in facilitates the re-use of LOs.

Table 2. LMS configuration course

	Included resources	Included LOs	Time to configure	Total time to configure	Available LOs
Course 1	3	3	00:02:18	00:08:30	1
Course 2	1	0	00:00:58	00:04:30	All LOs available in the repository

Regarding student interactions with the plug-in ILOIR, we evaluated the access of three students with different levels of understanding of the Social Security Law topics (poor, average and good), according to results of Table 3.

Table 3. ILOIR students' interaction

Student	Partial concept	Number of subjects demonstrated	Student's attention time	Number of wrong answers	Extra LOs (reinforcement)
1	Good	1	00:09:46	0	0
2	Average	2	00:21:13	3	1
3	Poor	3	00:34:19	6	3

Note that, depending on the student's performance, as measured by the number of errors made in the assessment within the LO and by delays in interacting with the object, additional new LOs are displayed to the student in the same learning session. This behavior represents the dynamic adaptation of the LO content provided by the system, as resolved by the agents (intelligent tier), according to student performance.

Figure 8 shows the point in time (t1) during the display of the LO related to Unit 2 of the diagnosis where it is signaled to Student 3 that a new LO will be presented. Figure 9 depicts the next step (t2) i.e. the presentation of a new LO whose topic (Unit 1) is a prerequisite to the subject of the previous LO.

The next section presents some discussions about our proposal.

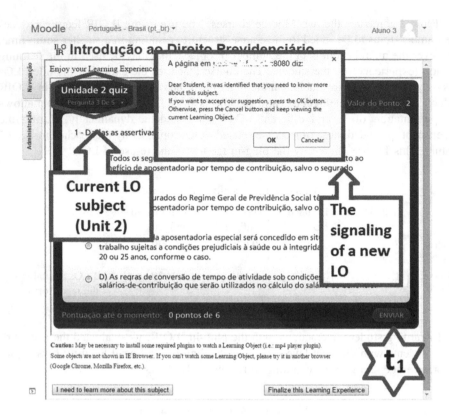

Fig. 8. Diagnosis and signaling the new LO to the Student 3, at LO related to Unit 2 (t1)

7   Discussions

This section discusses the potential benefits of the ILOMAS and the results of the experiments described above.

One of the ILOMAS' features that provides an improvement when compared to similar models (the ones presented in the Sect. 2) is the use of data from the interaction between the student and the learning resource.

As described above, the main focus of the ILOAgent is the interaction between the student and the learning object, within a LMS course. The monitoring of this interaction during the learning session makes it possible to identify the students' performance, dynamically, and thus to give a faster feedback. So it is not necessary to wait until the end of the learning session to see a sequence of errors in some test within the LO, for example, and realize that the student is getting into trouble with the current learning resource. If this is happening the ILOAgent can act in real time to improve the understanding of the student in that subject.

The model also facilitates the re-use of learning resources because teachers and instructional designers do not need to preconfigure the course's environment with all of the objects for each kind of student. ILOMAS takes into consideration data from the

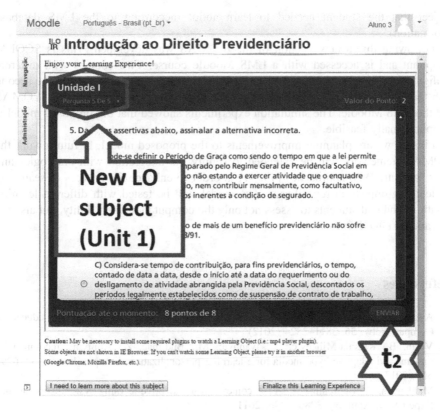

Fig. 9. Provision of the prerequisite LO (Unit 1) (t2)

LMS and from the LO (metadata) to better choose the specific learning resource to be presented to the student.

The next section presents the conclusions of this paper, and points out some areas for future work.

8 Conclusions and Future Work

This paper presented a model for building more adaptive and reusable educational experiences compared to alternative approaches. The ILOMAS framework was designed to allow dynamic LO selection on LMS courses, as an improvement of ILO's previous approach. The agents are modeled based on the practical reasoning paradigm (towards goal achievement). The MAS was developed following the Jadex BDI V3 framework which enables the agents' functionalities to be accessed as services. The use of Servlet technology provides the integration of the front-end and the intelligent tier.

A prototype was implemented to verify the proposed model and some evaluation tests were executed. In these the ILOMAS successfully received the learning experience requested by the student and identified dynamically an LO associated with the subject that the student needed to learn about (according to the LMS database information).

Following this a new version of the ILOMAS was developed. This is SCORM compliant and is accessed with a LMS Moodle course. Two courses with different configurations were simulated. The first with standard LMS resources and the second with the ILOIR plug-in — an artifact that enables integration between the ILOMAS and the LMS Moodle. The simulation experiments showed that the proposed model is computationally feasible.

Finally, we are planning improvements to the proposed model. In future work the ILOMAS framework will be extended to supply the integration with ontologies and other semantic Web approaches [40, 41] in order to enhance the process of searching for learning objects in repositories. The model will be tested with different learning situations and real students to assess not only the computational feasibility, but also the educational effectiveness.

References

1. Allison, C., Miller, A., Oliver, I., Michaelson, R., Tiropanis, T.: The web in education. Comput. Netw. **56**, 3811–3824 (2012)
2. Vesin, B., Klasnja-Milicevic, A., Ivanovic, M., Budimac, Z.: Applying recommender systems and adaptive hypermedia for e-learning personalization. Comput. Inform. **32**, 629–659 (2013)
3. Mahkameh, Y., Bahreininejad, A.: A context-aware adaptive learning system using agents. Expert Syst. Appl. **38**, 3280–3286 (2011)
4. Bachari, E., Abelwahed, E., Adnani, M.: E-learning personalization based on dynamic learners' preference. Int. J. Comp. Sci. Inform. Technol. (IJCSIT) **3**(3) (2011)
5. Caeiro, M., Llamas, M., Anido, L.: PoEML: modeling learning units through perspectives. Comput. Stand. Interfaces **36**, 380–396 (2014)
6. Santos, G., Jorge, J.: Interoperable intelligent tutoring systems as open educational resources. IEEE Trans. Learn. Technol. **6**(3), 271–282 (2013)
7. Despotovic-Zrakic, M., Markovic, A., Bogdanovic, Z., Barac, D., Krco, S.: Providing adaptivity in Moolde LMS courses. Educ. Technol. Soc. **15**(1), 326–338 (2012)
8. Kostolanyova, K., Sarmanova, J., Takacs, O.: Adaptation of teaching process based on a students individual learning needs. J. Effi. Responsib. Edu. Sci. **4**(1), 3–17 (2011)
9. Wiley, D.: Connecting learning objects to instructional design theory: a definition, a metaphor, and a taxonomy. Utah State University, Logan (2000). http://reusability.org/read/chapters/wiley.doc
10. Komlenov, Z., Budimac, Z., Ivanovic, M.: Introducing adaptivity features to a regular learning management system to support creation of advanced elessons. Inform. Educ. **9**(1), 63–80 (2010)
11. Barak, M., Ziv, S.: Wandering: a web-based platform for the creation of location-based interactive learning objects. Comput. Educ. **62**, 159–170 (2013)
12. Prometheus Design Tool (Eclipse Plug-in). https://code.google.com/p/pdt-plugin/
13. Pokahr, A., Braubach, L., Jander, K.: The Jadex project: programming model. In: Jarvis, D., Jarvis, J., Rönnquist, R., Jain, L.C. (eds.) Multiagent Systems and Applications. ISRL, vol. 46, pp. 21–53. Springer, Heidelberg (2013)

14. Jadex. http://www.activecomponents.org/bin/view/About/Features
15. Silva, J., Silveira, R.: The development of intelligent learning objects with an ontology based on the SCORM Standard. In: Seventh International Conference on Intelligent Systems Design and Applications, pp. 211–216. IEEE (2007)
16. SCORM: Advanced Distributed Learning (2004). http://www.adlnet.org/scorm
17. Chen, C.: Intelligent web-based learning system with personalized learning path guidance. Comput. Educ. **51**, 787–814 (2008)
18. Kurilovas, E., Zilinskiene, I., Dagiene, V.: Recommending suitable scenarios according to learners' preferences: an improved swarm based approach. Comput. Hum. Behav. **30**, 550–557 (2014)
19. Wooldridge, M., Jennings, N.: Intelligent agents: theory and practice. Knowl. Eng. Rev. **10** (2), 115–152 (1995)
20. Wooldridge, M.: An Introduction to Multi-agent Systems. Wiley, Chichester (2009)
21. Weiss, G.: Multi-agent Systems: A Modern Approach to Distributed Artificial Intelligence. The MIT Press, London (1999)
22. Pokahr, A., Braubach, L., Haubeck, C., Ladiges, J.: Programming BDI agents with pure Java. In: Müller, J.P., Weyrich, M., Bazzan, A.L.C. (eds.) MATES 2014. LNCS, vol. 8732, pp. 216–233. Springer, Heidelberg (2014)
23. MOODLE – Modular Oriented-Object Dynamic Learning Environment. http://moodle.org
24. Alencar, M., Netto, J.: Improving cooperation in virtual learning environments using multi-agent systems and AIML. In: 41st ASEE/IEEE Frontiers in Education Conference, Session, pp. F4C:1–6. IEEE (2011)
25. Giuffra, P., Silveira, R.: A multi-agent system model to integrate virtual learning environments and intelligent tutoring systems. Int. J. Interact. Multimedia Artif. Intell. **2** (1), 51–58 (2013)
26. Brown, E., Cristea, A., Stewart, C., Brailsford, T.: Patterns in authoring of adaptive educational hypermedia: a taxonomy of learning styles. Educ. Technol. Soc. **8**(3), 77–90 (2005)
27. Moura, F., Fernandes, M.: A proposal of computational model which uses PSO for choosing learning objects based on the Kolb spiral and the multiple intelligences. In: XXIII Informatics in Education Brazilian Symposium (SBIE) (2012)
28. Carvalho, V., Dorça, F., Cattelan, R., Araújo, R.: An approach to automatic and dynamic recommendation of learning objects based on learning styles. In: XXV Informatics in Education Brazilian Symposium (SBIE) (2014)
29. Bremgartner, V., Netto, J., Menezes, C.: Using agents and open student model ontology to provide adaptation of constructivist contents in virtual learning environments. In: XXV Informatics in Education Brazilian Symposium (SBIE) (2014)
30. Pereira, C., Campos, F., Ströele, V., David, J., Braga, R.: Extraction of profile and context features in social networks for recommendation of learning resources. In: XXV Informatics in Education Brazilian Symposium (SBIE) (2014)
31. Frade, R, Neto, F., Lima, R.W., Lima, R.M., Silva, L., Souza, R.: A multi-agent 3D virtual environment with personalized recommendation of learning objects. In: XXV Informatics in Education Brazilian Symposium (SBIE) (2014)
32. Santos, R., Luz, B., Martins, V., Guimarães, M.: eTutor: an interactive learning environment. In: XXV Informatics in Education Brazilian Symposium (SBIE) (2014)
33. Silveira, R., Gomes, E., Vicari, R.: Intelligent learning objects: an agent-based approach to learning objects. Int. Fed. Inf. Process. **182**, 103–110 (2006)
34. Bavaresco, N., Silveira, R.: Proposal of an architecture to build intelligent learning objects based on BDI agents. In: XX Informatics in Education Brazilian Symposium (SBIE) (2009)

35. Padgham, L., Winikoff, M.: Developing Intelligent Agent Systems – A Practical Guide. Wiley, Chichester (2004)
36. Braubach, L., Pokahr, A.: Jadex active components framework – BDI agents for disaster rescue coordination. Softw. Agents Agent Syst. Appl. **32**, 57–84 (2012)
37. Gamma, E., Helm, R., Johnson, R., Vlissides, J.: Design Patterns: Elements of Reusable Object-Oriented Software. Addison-Wesley, Amsterdam (1995)
38. Morrison, M.: Head First JavaScript. O'Reilly, Sebastopol (2008)
39. Braubach, L., Pokahr, A.: Developing distributed systems with active components and Jadex. Scalable Comput. Pract. Experience **13**(2), 3–24 (2012)
40. de-Marcos, L., Pages, C., Martinez, J., Gutierrez, J.: Competency-based learning object sequencing using particle swarms. In: 19th IEEE International Conference on Tools with Artificial Intelligence - ICTAI, vol. 2, pp. 111–116 (2007)
41. Santos, E.R., Boff, E., Vicari, R.M.: Semantic web technologies applied to interoperability on an educational portal. In: Ikeda, M., Ashley, K.D., Chan, T.-W. (eds.) ITS 2006. LNCS, vol. 4053, pp. 308–317. Springer, Heidelberg (2006)

The Socio-Cultural Approach to Software Engineering and its Application to Modeling a Virtual Learning Environment

João Carlos Gluz[1]([✉]), Rosa Maria Vicari[2], and Liliana M. Passerino[2]

[1] Post-Graduate Program in Applied Computing (PIPCA), UNISINOS, São Leopoldo, RS, Brazil
jcgluz@unisinos.br
[2] Interdisciplinary Center for Educational Technologies (CINTED), UFRGS,
Porto Alegre, RS, Brazil
rosa@inf.ufrgs.br, liliana@cinted.ufrgs.br

Abstract. Sociability, autonomy and intelligence are becoming important properties of new mobile and web applications. Sociability is the main reason for the development of these new applications, while autonomy and intelligence are necessary skills to support sociability's requirements. This is also true in the educational software area, where educational applications intermediate the interaction among students and teachers, and are increasingly intelligent and autonomous. Aiming to help in the development of this new kind of software, this work presents the Socio-Cultural Approach to Software Engineering (SCASE), a proposal for the design and development of software systems as social and cultural artifacts. It introduces SCASE with a simple scenario commonly used to exemplify multi-agent systems. The work finishes with the modeling of an innovative educational application formed by a virtual learning environment extended with semantic services for learning objects, which can recognize the semantics of these objects.

1 Introduction

This work introduces the Socio-Cultural Approach to Software Engineering (SCASE) that offer a perspective for the design and development of software systems aligned with properties such as Sociability, Autonomy and Intelligence. These properties have become increasingly important in design and development of new applications. Sociability is the main reason for the development of these applications. The main advantage offered by new "social-like" applications is to provide communication between people and help them to establish relationships with participants of the digital social context created by the application. Autonomy becomes obligatory when one considers the universe of new users being reached by these applications. The majority of these users does not know or have no interest in explicitly learning on how to use any computer resource. Typical users only want to use the digital device to communicate and be noticed in social contexts, they do not want to understand how the device or the digital communication works. Intelligence comes in the wake of sociability and autonomy: autonomous systems and applications with really good social skills must have a certain level of

© Springer International Publishing Switzerland 2016
F. Koch et al. (Eds.): SOCIALEDU 2015, CCIS 606, pp. 83–103, 2016.
DOI: 10.1007/978-3-319-39672-9_7

intelligence. This phenomenon also occurs in the educational software area. Educational applications such as Virtual Learning Environments (VLE) are not simple storage facilities for educational contents, but actively intermediate the digital interaction among students and teachers. These environments are increasingly becoming intelligent and autonomous, to simplify the tasks of students and teachers.

The conception, design and development of a given software system has always been a social construction process. In this context, the SCASE can help to clarify and highlight the social and cultural aspects of this process. According to the SCASE approach, a software application or system should be viewed from the beginning as a social and cultural artifact, both in its design, development and use. Software applications are inventions or constructions created by members of a given society and culture. In the context considered in this work, either the form of use or the value of these applications is determined by social and cultural norms, which should be incorporated in such artifacts. In the same way, these software artifacts also help to establish and maintain social and cultural norms. From a user's point of view, these applications are becoming more than tools that bring a particular functionality for an individual user, but are instead a medium or vehicle for communication that is shared among its users. Traditional functional software features become aggregated values over mediated communication.

To illustrate SCASE concepts, the present work shows two study cases: an introductory gold miners scenario commonly used to exemplify multi-agent systems [6, 9], and an educational application scenario, intended to model the main features of a semantic platform for learning objects integrated with a VLE. The educational application was selected because it is a new and complex application, which requires the main capabilities of SCASE to be modeled. This application is derived from previous works with pedagogical agents, tutoring systems, intelligent virtual environments and educational ontologies [11, 21]. Indeed, SCASE is a major evolution from our previous work on software engineering methods derived from Intelligent Tutoring Systems (ITS) practices [20].

2   Related Work

SCASE is aligned with works that study the application of social models to requirements engineering [30], particularly on the researches about social oriented software engineering methodologies [7, 8, 12]. It has several intersecting features with TROPOS methodology [8]. SCASE and TROPOS are profoundly influenced by i* models and techniques [29, 31]. However, SCASE and TROPOS differ in some important aspects: SCASE extends i* to handle cultural contexts and provides a tighter integration with UML 2.0. There are some ideas from other works that helped to shape SCASE, especially on the possible mapping from i* models to UML diagrams. The work of [17] shows that is possible to transform agent's plans into UML's Activity diagrams, justifying our approach to convert i* rationalization plans (or routines) in this kind of UML diagram. In SCASE the guidelines presented in [7], can be used to map i* models into UML Class diagrams representing i* artificial agents. The main difference with this work, is that the guidelines presented in [7] cannot handle the new cultural and ontological elements proposed for i* diagrams.

The semantic platform for learning objects, used as the main study case for SCASE methods, is related to the application of agents, ontologies and Learning Objects (LO) to design and development of educational systems. Recent examples of the application of gent-based technology on educational systems are the works [1, 4, 18]. Most of the works on agents are focused on the ITS and VLE perspectives, not intersecting with the LO semantic repository perspective considered in this work. The application of agent technology for LO is more promising [19], however this work does not take into account the requirements and questions related to LO repositories. Works on the application of ontologies in education [3, 21] were generally more interested on the impact and benefits of this technology on learning environments, exploring how ontologies could represent learning domains, educational applications, students profile, curricular structure and similar issues. The relation with our work is irregular, being more predominant when issues related to learning contents are considered.

3   SCASE Tasks and Tools

In SCASE, the analysis, design, development and validation phases or stages of software engineering processes are divided in following tasks:

- *Analysis:* the analysis process of the social environment and cultural context where the software application will participate and interact.
- *Synthesis:* the design process of the conceptual and dynamic architectural software models.
- *Construction:* the collaborative and teamwork based development of software artifacts.
- *Experimentation*: the empirical experimentation of software models and software artifacts, which must be based on qualitative or quantitative scientific methods.

The requirements specification of the application domain equates with the SCASE phase of the analysis of the social environment in which the application will participate as another social actor, and the analysis of the cultural context where this application, as a social actor, will need to understand and interact. This analysis seeks to highlight and identify the social relationships among their various participants, regardless of whether they are human actors, institutions or software systems (artificial agents). The collection of social relationships that rely on the capacities of the software application to produce some useful work or result, essentially define the requirements of the application in usual software engineering terminology.

Cultural aspects can be critical for the success of analysis. Among other things, a culture defines a network of meanings shared by each participant in this culture in their social interactions. Without a shared culture, communication can become meaningless because there is no shared semantics. Thus, in addition to the social relationships, cultural contexts are considered crucial to the success of the analysis, providing the meaning and form for the interactions that occur in social relationships.

The analysis produces a model of the social environment of the application, able to represent the relationship of dependency between the actors of the scenario, the cultural contexts in which these relationships are established and the intentions, goals and rationale that actors have behind the relationships. Section 3.1 presents the tool proposed in SCASE to create these models.

This socio-cultural model provides the basis for the synthesis of the architectural models of the software. This synthesis process results in the creation of architectural models of software that include conceptual models and dynamic models. Conceptual models will specify things like the organization of the multi-agent system, the architecture of individual agents and the ontology of the application domain (shared culture), while dynamic models will specify the interactions that can occur between agents, and how agents behave in respect to these interactions. The tools used to create the conceptual and dynamic models used in SCASE are presented in Sect. 3.2.

Later, these models are the basis for the software construction process that results in the implementation of agents that make up the multi-agent system architecture. The key points here, in terms of SCASE, are the strong reliance on multi-agent and agent based paradigms for software development [25, 28], and the commitment to collaborative and teamwork centered approach to software development.

The process of software validation and verification is the complement of the synthesis process. In SCASE, validation is considered from the perspective of the scientific method. From this perspective, the models and systems resulting from the synthesis represent a concrete model on phenomena of reality that must be put to the test by experiments designed from the perspective of the scientific method. Here Popper's concept of *falsifiability* [16] fits perfectly: in logical terms it simply does not make sense to *validate* a given model, at least if this implies a guarantee that this model will be true in *all* possible situations. What can be expected is that the application's models are scientific, that is, they can be put to tests or experiments that conceivably will result false (i.e., they can be *falsifiable* in Popper's terminology). In this perspective, the software artifact resulting from the construction process is a concrete computational model that can be experimentally tested. The process of experimentation of the software aims to expose the flaws and defects of the several models that comprise it. Rigorous experimental protocols and procedures, whether quantitative or qualitative, are needed to ensure the reliability of the results of the experiments.

3.1 The Proposed Analysis Tool

The analysis tool proposed in SCASE is based on i* modeling tool for social systems analysis [29, 31], which can represent organizational aspects involved in social processes, describing motivations and intentionality aspects of actors in organizational environments. These environments are characterized as social systems (institutions, organizations, companies), in which actors are committed to work cooperatively. The Strategic Dependencies (SD) diagrams of i* model dependency relations between actors, while Strategic Reasons (SR) diagrams, represent the motivations and intentions of the actors in respect to its dependencies (Fig. 1(b)). SD diagrams are composed by nodes that represent actors and links, which represent dependencies among actors (Fig. 1(a)).

Actors are entities that perform actions in order to achieve goals in the environment. Simple circle nodes represent actors and circle nodes with a horizontal bar at the top are specializations of actors in the form of artificial agents. Dependencies motivated by "hard" goals are represented by oval rectangles, dependencies related to tasks are represented by hexagons, dependencies for resources are represented by rectangles and dependencies by "soft" goals are represented by oval with indentations. SR diagrams allow a detailed definition of plans (or routines, following i* terminology [29]) associated with the relations of dependence under the responsibility of some actor (Fig. 1(b)).

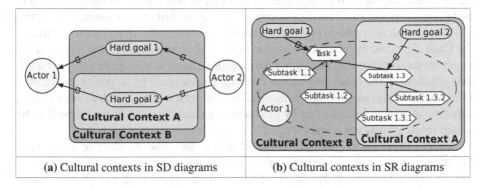

(a) Cultural contexts in SD diagrams	(b) Cultural contexts in SR diagrams

Fig. 1. Notation used to specify cultural contexts in SD (a) and SR (b) diagrams.

The i* technique was not created to model cultural aspects of social relations of dependence, assumed as necessary for the complete characterization of a software as a sociocultural artifact. Culture is an important part of any society or social system, but the definition of this concept encompasses a wide continuum of options. This work aims to give a reasonable (or, at least, defensible) software engineering interpretation to some aspects of culture concept, assuming that culture is, as defined in relation to anthropological studies, "the set of shared attitudes, values, goals, and practices that characterizes an institution or organization" [13]. As a consequence, the cultural context defines form, meaning and value of shared information in a social relationship. Culture should materialize the meanings (semantics) of the goals, tasks and shared resources in dependency relationships, and the form (syntax) how these elements can be expressed and communicated from some actor to another. Given these premises, the cultural context assumes a precise function in terms of i* models. This context defines the languages and protocols of social interactions derived or implied by the dependency relationships. This context also defines the ontology, which gives meaning to the terms of this language. The meaning of each goal, task or shared resource should be specified by a particular element of this ontology. In the proposed i* extension, a cultural context is represented by drawing a rectangle with rounded corners bellow the diagram elements encompassed by that culture. Figure 1 shows main elements of this extension.

A diagram can contain more than one cultural context, in which case the corresponding rectangles may be separated indicating independent cultures, or they can overlap indicating that the corresponding cultures share some common elements (ontology languages or protocols). Elements, be they actors, goals, tasks or resources in areas where there are two or more overlapping cultures must have equivalent meanings in both cultures.

3.2   The Architectural Modeling Tools

The Unified Modeling Language (UML) offers standard modeling tools to visualize, specify, design, and document software systems [14]. Use case diagrams of UML are not necessary in SCASE, because the SD and SR diagrams of i* substitute entirely the use case diagrams of UML, with several important benefits. Besides being oriented to model the social and (with our extension) cultural aspects of some system, i* diagrams provide a complete graphical notation for requirements specification. This is not true of Use Case diagrams: the graphical notation of these diagrams is only a small part of the requirements specification, the biggest part is hidden in textual descriptions, or in unrelated notations: "The behavior of a use case can be described by a specification that is some kind of Behavior (through its *ownedBehavior* relationship), such as interactions, activities, and state machines, or by pre-conditions and post-conditions as well as by natural language text where appropriate." [14; p. 596].

Starting from 2.0 version, UML included diagrams like Activity and Sequence diagrams, which can model dynamic aspects of multi-agent systems. These diagrams are used in SCASE to create dynamic models of software systems [2, 27]. These dynamic models can be derived from i* requirements diagrams, but, to do so it is necessary to understand the dynamics behind the social relationships of i* models. A dialectical assumption underlies our approach: a social relationship implies and at the same time depends on the social interactions that occur between actors involved in some relationship. These interactions lead to the exchange of messages between actors. As a consequence, Communication and Sequence diagrams can specify messages and interaction protocols behind dependency relations.

The intentionality of agents, modeled by the decomposition of relations of dependence on plans under the responsibility of the agent, leads to a dynamic model formed by the execution of the actions of these plans. Following [17], SCASE assumes that Activity diagrams will model the process of functional decomposition defined in SR diagrams. To let the UML diagrams more compatible with i* notation, some minor syntax sugaring was allowed in these UML diagrams, using the symbols for agents and software entities of i* to represent lifelines of Communication and Sequence diagrams. The same form of representation of cultural contexts proposed to i* can be used in UML diagrams. Ontologies are represented by colored rounded rectangles that can be placed in any UML diagram. If some ontology encloses the lifeline of a Communication or Sequence diagram, then this lifeline entity will use the ontology to give meaning to its interactions with other lifelines. Thus, communication links connected to a lifeline that pass over some ontology rectangle, contain messages related to this ontology. Similarly, if the ontology encloses some event or signal action of Activity diagrams, then the meaning of the message related to the event is defined by the ontology. If some ontology is enclosed inside other ontology, then the enclosing ontology provides terms and relations used in the enclosed ontology.

Besides the dynamic model, the class hierarchy of the software entities and objects belonging to the system forms another important architectural model of any system. This is called the conceptual model of the system, which describes the properties of the software entities and objects of the system in an abstract way, showing how these descriptions can be organized in class hierarchies. The conceptual model can be represented by Class diagrams of UML or OWL ontologies [24].

4   The Gold Miners Scenario

The gold miners scenario is a classical study case for multi-agent systems. It was used in the contest realized in the seventh Computational Logic in Multi-Agent Systems (CLIMA) workshop [9]. It is also used as an implementation example for Agent-Speak(L) agent programming language and JASON development environment [5].

4.1   Social Dependencies

The first step in the analysis of a given social scenario is constituted by the identification of what are the main characters or actors involved in this scenario. In the gold miners scenario a gold rush occurs in a determined region. Miners are pouring in the region to find the maximum quantity of gold nuggets dispersed in the area. The area is divided in quadrants, which are subdivided in cells. The computational version works with teams of gold miners robots, divided into team leaders and miners. The SD model for this scenario is presented on Fig. 2.

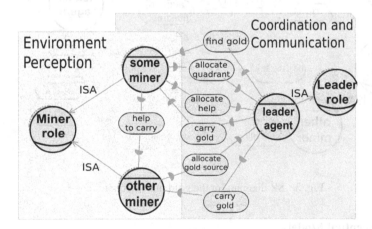

Fig. 2. SD diagram for the gold miners robots scenario

In the SD diagram of Fig. 2 robots are represented by artificial agents divided in two different roles: the leader of miner teams, and the miner robots themselves. The leader depends on miners to find and carry gold, and miners depend on team leader for allocation tasks. There is also a minor variation, depending on the state of some miner: if this miner found lots of gold, and cannot carry all of them then the leader robot will try to find some other miner robots to help the lucky robot. Two cultural contexts are also identified in this diagram, related to the roles of each robot. The environment perceptions context, define the knowledge (meaning) of the things that can be found in the environment. The coordination and communication context defines the meaning of the information the coordination of teams of robots.

4.2 Rationalization Model

The SD diagram of Fig. 2 is refined in the SR diagram of Fig. 3. In this diagram specific tasks are assigned to each miner to handle its responsibilities in respect to the social dependencies specified in the SD diagram. Besides registering and storing gold found by miners, the leader agent will need to execute the allocation of initial quadrants and also found helpers if necessary. Note that for pedagogical purposes it was used a very simple multi-agent coordination model, which assumes that the leader agent will decide if some helper is necessary, based on information passes by miners and the current distribution of miners in the area.

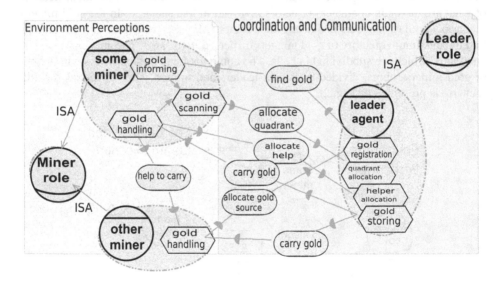

Fig. 3. SR diagram for the gold miners robot scenario.

4.3 Conceptual Models

The SD and SR diagrams for the gold miners scenario provide enough information to start the architectural synthesis process. In first place, is necessary to specify the conceptual models for the artificial agents that control (or simulate) the miner robots, and the cultural contexts where these agents are inserted. The conceptual model defines the properties of the software entities and objects of the system in an abstract way, showing how these descriptions can be organized in formal ontologies or in software-based class hierarchies. In SCASE, the properties of the artificial agents of i* diagrams can be defined through UML Class diagrams derived directly from information already available on this diagrams. Guidelines presented in [7] already show how to map i* models in UML Class diagrams to define the classes of i* artificial agents.

However, the guidelines presented in [7] cannot handle the new cultural contexts proposed in SCASE for i* diagrams. Conceptual elements of these contexts are handled by an ontological approach. These elements define the underlying meaning behind the goals and interactions implied by social dependencies, and can be best defined by an ontology described in a formal language like OWL.

Returning to the gold miners scenario, the Coordination and Communication context, identified in the SD diagram of Fig. 2, should define the meaning of all information to be exchanged between agents to fulfill social dependencies. The OWL ontology proposed for this context is presented in Fig. 4(b), defining specific classes for each one of these dependencies. The Environment Perceptions context is related to the individual perceptions of each agent, so it is not so directly captured by the dependencies in a SD diagram (unless something similar to an "environment" actor is created in this diagram). The OWL ontology proposed in Fig. 4(a) defines the basic elements that can be identified in the environment and conceivably impact in the tasks to be executed by the agent. This includes, the position the robot is located, the corresponding cell, if there are evidence of gold in this cell, if there are other miner working in the same cell and if the miner is carrying some gold.

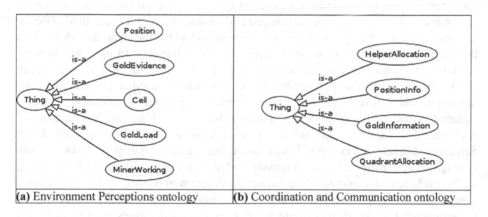

(a) Environment Perceptions ontology   (b) Coordination and Communication ontology

Fig. 4. Ontologies for the cultural contexts identified in the gold miners SD diagram

The categorization of agents in miner and leader roles defined in the gold miners SD diagram (Fig. 2) is modeled in the class diagram presented in Fig. 5. The guidelines proposed in [7] allow to map some elements of i* models to UML Class diagrams. Following these guidelines the tasks defined in the SR diagram on Fig. 5, are modeled as methods of the class. However, the guidelines presented in [7] cannot handle the new cultural and ontological elements proposed in SCASE for i* diagrams. To solve this, in the class diagram presented in Fig. 5 the information represented in the cultural context, as defined by the ontologies on Fig. 4, are

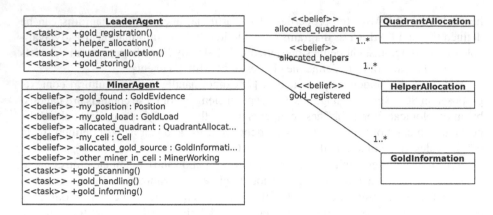

Fig. 5. Class diagram for the leader and miner roles

modeled as the *beliefs* of these agents, which are attributes or relation that store provisional information maintained by the agent.

4.4 Dynamic Models

To model the dynamic aspects of some system new tools and guidelines are necessary. These tools and guidelines will orient how social dependencies and rationalization plans of i* diagrams can be mapped in dynamic models. A dialectical assumption underlies SCASE approach: relationships imply and at the same time depend on the social interactions that occur between the actors involved in the relationships. Social interactions will lead to the exchange of messages and knowledge between actors. From a cultural perspective these interactions need a (communication) language, and usually follow common interaction patterns (a protocol). Thus a dynamic model of the system will specify who communicates with whom, using which kind of language and following what kind of interaction protocol. UML Sequence diagrams offer a good start, modeling the communication links existing among software entities, the main messages that flow in these links and the ordering in the exchange of messages. The Sequence diagram presented in Fig. 6, shows a possible model for the interactions behind the social dependencies in the gold miners scenario (see Fig. 2). In this Sequence diagram, named frames or protocol fragments are used to document how some particular interaction is correlated with the correspondent social dependence defined in the SD diagram of Fig. 2. With this is not necessary to define any "goal" method in some agent class, but only to identify how some particular task method will react to the communication events defined in the Sequence diagram.

To see how this modeling works, the Activity diagram presented in Fig. 7, shows how the *allocation_quadrant* task method behavior is modeled.

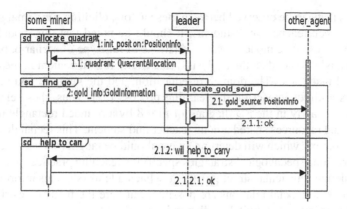

Fig. 6. Sequence diagram for the gold miners scenario

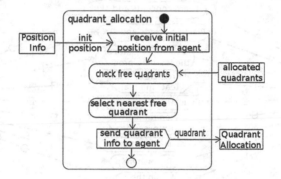

Fig. 7. Behavior of the *quadrant_allocation* task method.

5   The Educational Application Scenario

The analysis and synthesis phases of SCASE approach will also be illustrated by an educational scenario based on a semantic content platform specialized to provide Learning Objects (LO) [15, 26]. The requirements analysis process will observe and detail the social relationships these entities have with other actors in an educational scenario and the impact of these relationships with the activities involved in the life cycle of LO. Then, it will follow a synthesis process, which aims to produce architectural models based on the generalization of ontologies, social relationships and plans elicited in the requirements analysis.

5.1   Social Dependencies

Two main actors were initially considered in the educational application scenario: the *student* who is the focus of the case and the actor who is expected to have the biggest gain in terms of learning, and the *teacher* who is responsible for planning, teaching and also the evaluation of this process. Figure 8 shows an SD diagram of the main social relationships that can be observed between these actors, eliciting a minimal set of relationships between teachers and students. It should be noted that this model does not purport to be a complete model of social relations of this type of scenario, but only an appropriate model to conduct the analysis of the use of digital content in the context of technological mediation. The domain of education, and the methods and practices of teaching has a direct impact on the learning process [32]. Thus, these elements are represented abstractly in the SD diagram of Fig. 8 by a rounded rectangle underlying goals, tasks and resources shared among teacher and student. This rectangle represents the cultural context, which will determine what should be taught (the learning domain), how it will be done (pedagogical strategies specifying teaching practices and methods), in which ordering (curricular structure) and to what students (students information). As noted before, other social relations are possible, but here the focus is restricted to an educational scenario when digital mediation is introduced.

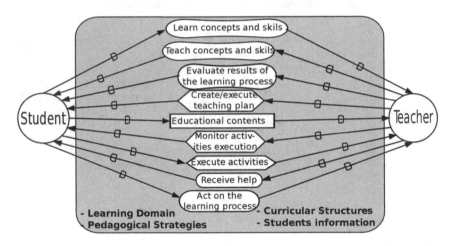

Fig. 8. SD model for teacher + student scenario

The model on Fig. 8 proposes as soft goals of the teaching process: the dependence that students have on teachers to learn the concepts and skills of the learning domain, considering teachers as more experienced peers in mediating [22, 23] and the dependencies that teachers have towards their students to achieve their goals of teaching concepts and skills, and to evaluate the results of this process. Two hard goals of this model are also directly related to the educational process: students depend on the assistance and help of teachers, but teachers also depend on students to teach (i.e. to act on the learning process). These goals are critical to the process of teaching and human actors should always be responsible to achieve them. Both goals can be functionally decomposed into actions that can be observed or recorded, showing, for instance, if a help request has been met, or when a given teaching action occurred. This kind of results will not be modeled as concrete goals, but are related to analysis of previously viewed nonfunctional goals. Finally, students depend on teachers for specific materials about the learning domain and teaching and pedagogical activities that occur throughout the educational process.

The SD diagram of Fig. 9 shows what happens when a third element is introduced in this context, leading from the interaction of a classroom setting to a distance learning mode of education mediated by a Virtual Learning Environment (VLE). The diagram of Fig. 9 models the dependencies of a generic VLE, identifying the necessary dependencies to ensure consistency with the model outlined in Fig. 8. Now the tasks to develop and provide educational activities and materials, the starting and monitoring of the learning process and the interaction with students shall undergo a process of digital mediation by the VLE. Educational materials become digital materials available to the student in digital media.

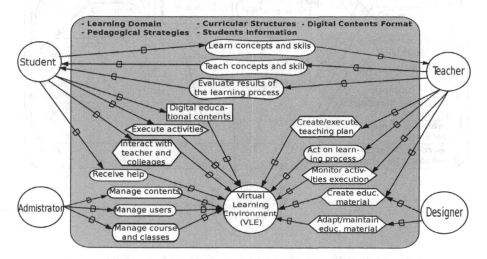

Fig. 9. SD model for student + teacher + VLE scenario

Likewise the various didactic and pedagogical activities that must occur to the educational process right now must be performed with the aid of the VLE. This leads to some form of representation of these digital contents, indicated in the diagram of Fig. 2 by the "Digital Contents Formats" cultural context. The VLE enters as an instrument to support digital mediation, providing tools to perform tasks previously conducted face to face. When the VLE enters the scene, other actors also appear, including the figure of the VLE administrator and also the designer of digital content (which can even be a specialized role of teachers).

The diagram in Fig. 9 is not the final SD diagram for this complex educational scenario. The model presented in Fig. 10, shows what goals, common tasks and features are affected when the VLE is integrated with a Semantic Platform for Learning Objects (SPLO). The SPLO can be used as a standalone tool or can be integrated to some VLE. Because VLEs are, at least in respect to formal education, the most widespread interface to access educational material, this scenario assumes that the SPLO is integrated to the VLE.

Figure 10 summarizes the analysis of the situation, identifying the main actors of this scenario and their respective goals, tasks and shared resources. This diagram identifies key goals and resources shared across a hypothetical VLE and the SPLO. In SCASE

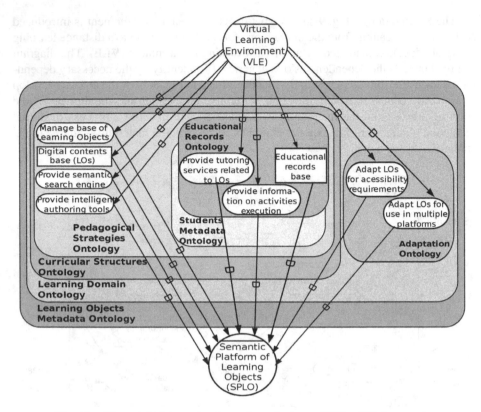

Fig. 10. SD model of dependencies and ontologies on VLE + SPLO scenario

approach it is important to define the semantics of the social interactions underlying the dependency relationships. Therefore, the i* extension proposed in Sect. 3.1 was used in its full extent to show how the set of ontologies implied by the cultural context presented in Fig. 9 should be divided in specific ontologies and how these ontologies are related to the social dependencies between the VLE and the semantic contents platform. Such ontologies are represented in the extended SD diagrams presented in Fig. 10, using colored rectangles drawn under greater dependency relationships. The semantic context of a dependency relationship is defined by ontologies located under the symbol of the relationship.

5.2 Refinements and Rationalization Models

After actors, social dependencies and general cultural contexts have been identified in SD diagrams, is possible either to refine actors that are institutions or software systems or to proceed to the creation of rationalization models (SR diagrams) that show the plans these actors have to satisfy the dependencies under their responsibility. This Section will show examples of both options.

First an example of SR diagram, showing a rationale that can be ascribed to students, given the set of dependencies identified in SD diagram of Fig. 9. The SR diagram of Fig. 11 shows the decomposition of the goals, objectives and tasks outlined in the SD diagram in Fig. 9 in possible plans to be performed by the student. In this relatively simple model, the main intention ascribed to students is to achieve the learning goals of the learning domain. This goal is decomposed in three main tasks: to conduct the learning activities of the teaching plan, to identify problems occurring with these activities and seek help, and to interact with teacher and colleagues while doing this.

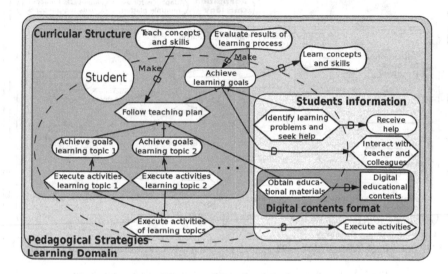

Fig. 11. A possible SR model for students

The "teach concepts and skills" soft goal of teachers can be satisfied if the student effectively follows the teaching plan (see the make dependency relationship). The teacher's soft goal to evaluate the results of the learning process will be satisfied if the student achieves the learning goals. The realization of the activities by the student is divided into goals and tasks related to the topics of the learning domain. To execute these activities and obtain the educational material related to them, the student will need to use the VLE. The set of cultural contexts identified in Fig. 9 where divided in Fig. 11, to cover specific goals, tasks or resources influenced by the cultural context.

The next examples show how to refine SD diagrams. If some particular actor is an institution or organization, then is possible to consider this "actor" as a new social environment and use SD diagrams to analyze and model it. This is also true for software systems conceived as composed by subsystems. This is an application of i* diagram refinement ideas used in TROPOS [8, 10]. The SD diagram in Fig. 12 shows how the semantic platform of learning objects can be refined into several systems. The life cycle of learning objects was the analysis unit used to elicit the services to be provided for users. Following [11], this life cycle was divided in the activities of authoring, search, use and maintenance. The organization of systems defined in Fig. 12 follows this division. The goal to provide intelligent authoring tools is part of the authoring activity. The goal to provide a semantic search engine is essential to search and locate an appropriate object. The goals to provide tutoring (pedagogical support) services and to monitor and provide information are the keys to provide a good support for the use of learning objects. Finally, the management of the base of LO and the adaptation of these objects for accessibility purposes or for multiple platforms requirements are goals of the maintenance phase.

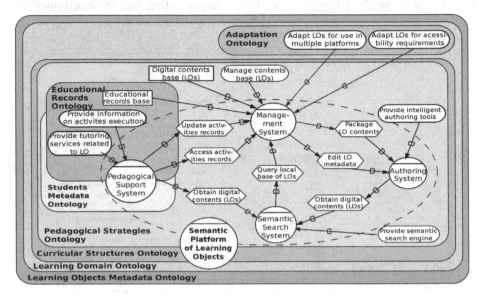

Fig. 12. SD diagram for the semantic platform of learning objects

The diagram presented in Fig. 13, is an example of SR model, showing how the Semantic Search system intends to attain goals and tasks under its responsibility.

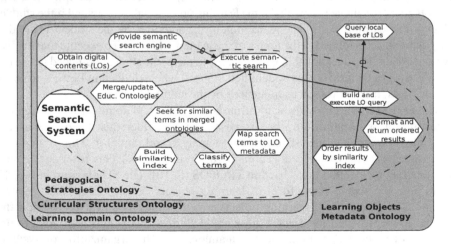

Fig. 13. SR model for the semantic search system.

The SR model in Fig. 13 show how the main task of this system is subdivided in several subtasks. In this system the several educational ontologies must be merged as a unique integrated ontology that provides the context for semantic searches. Terms similar or equivalent to the terms provided by the user are searched in the merged educational ontology. Because information about the contents to be searched are contained in learning object metadata, is necessary to map the search terms to appropriate metadata, when building a query for the learning object base.

5.3 Conceptual Models

Cultural contexts identified in Sects. 5.1 and 5.2 are important because they provide the semantics for the "semantic" platform. The structural model for the ontologies of the semantic platform is shown in Fig. 14, considers the requirements of the SR model for Semantic Search system (Fig. 13).

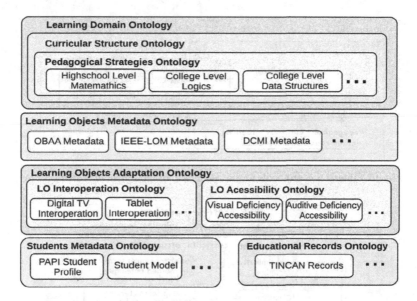

Fig. 14. Overall structure of the ontological model for VLE + SPLO integration

In this model, educational ontologies are structured in generalization levels, starting from the most general level formed by the Learner Domain ontology, which defines high-level classes of learning domains, passing by the Curricular Structure ontology that define general concepts related to curriculum of courses and disciplines, and reaching to the Pedagogical Strategies ontology that defines overall concepts related to strategies and methods for teaching subjects. Ontologies for specific disciplines should include general educational ontologies (the Learner Domain, Curricular Structure and Pedagogical Strategies ontologies), and specialize the higher-level concepts, classes and relationships defined in these ontologies. The knowledge represented in these ontologies allows the semantic search engine to understand the educational context where the learning object is being used. Authoring tools of the semantic platform can use the knowledge available in educational ontologies to help.

5.4 Dynamic Models

The models presented in previous Sections do not show the dynamics that make social relations, cultural contexts and ontologies to work. To create a computational model for the agents of these models is necessary to understand the dynamics behind social relationships. The dialectical assumption is that a social relationship implies and at the same time depends on social interactions between actors involved in the relationship. This leads to the exchange of messages between actors, requiring common languages and interaction protocols. The UML Sequence diagram, presented in Fig. 15, models the interaction protocols behind "Provide search engine" and "Query local base of LO" social dependences in the SR model of the semantic search system (see Fig. 13).

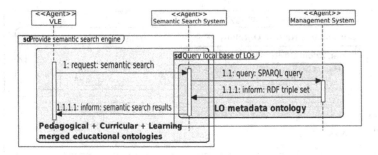

Fig. 15. Interaction protocols for the SR model of the semantic search system.

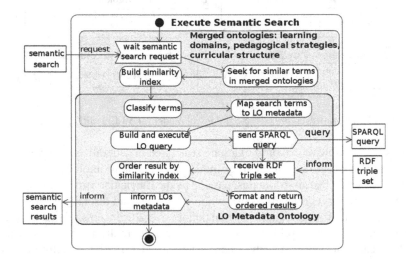

Fig. 16. Activity diagrams for the semantic search system.

The plans of i* agents contained in some SR diagrams can be modeled to any degree required by Activity diagrams of UML 2.0 [17]. Figure 16 shows an example of this case, detailing how the task "Execute semantic search" (see Fig. 13) is executed.

6   Conclusions

SCASE techniques still are in an evolving stage and the proposed extension of i* to represent cultural contexts should eventually be benefited by more rigorous or formal definitions. However, as it was introduced in this work, it is possible to use SCASE techniques to model important features of a relatively complex software application with clear social and cultural impacts. This kind of software application is a good example of new applications where sociability, autonomy and intelligence start to become key properties for its users. The fact that SCASE can be used productively to analyze and design one of these applications provides good evidence of the feasibility of this approach.

The requirements and architectural models for the semantic platform of educational contents proposed in this work are another important result. These models show how the social relationships between students and teachers evolve and adapt to digital mediated scenarios, with the inclusion of the VLE, followed by the integration with a semantic platform for educational contents. The models defined in Sect. 5 identify the requirements necessary for this kind of learning environment. They show how to combine the state of the art in agent, ontology and learning object technologies to build the basic services of a semantic repository for learning objects, properly integrated to a VLE. The work addresses how to integrate ontology and agent engineering to model this application. Nowadays, to our knowledge, there is no digital educational platform that can handle all of these features.

References

1. Arias, F., Moreno, J., Ovalle, D.: Integration model of e-learning based on pedagogical software agents and collaborative learning environments. In: Proceedings of IFIP World Conference on Computers in Education (WCCE), pp. 1–10 (2009)
2. Bauer, B., Odell, J.: UML 2.0 and agents: how to build agent-based systems with the new UML standard. Eng. Appl. Artif. Intell. **18**, 141–157 (2005)
3. Bittencourt, I., Costa, E., Silva, M., Soares, E.: A computational model for developing semantic web-based educational systems. Knowl.-Based Syst. **22**(4), 302–315 (2009)
4. Bittencourt, I., Costa, E.B., Neto, B.F.S., Menezes, J.G.M., Melo, J.S.S., Fernada, E., Silva, A.P, Brasil, L.M.: Constructing intelligent tutoring systems based on a multiagent architecture. In: Vicari, R.M., Jaques, P.A., Verdin, R. (eds.) Agent-Based Tutoring Systems by Cognitive and Affective Modeling, pp. 28–59. IGI Press (2008)
5. Bordini, R., Hübner, J.F., Wooldridge, M.: Programming Multi-Agent Systems in AgentSpeak Using Jason. Wiley Series in Agent Technology. Wiley, Hoboken (2007)
6. Bordini, R.II., Hubner, J.F., Vieira, R.: JASON and the golden fleece of agent-oriented programming. In: Bordini, R.H., Dastani, M., Dix, J., Seghrouchni, A.E.F. (eds.) Multi-Agent Programming: Languages, pp. 3–37. Springer, Heidelberg (2005)

7. Castro, J., Alencar, F., Santander, V., Silva, C.: Integration of i * and object-oriented models. In: Yu, E., Giorgini, P., Maiden, N., Mylopoulos, J. (eds.) Social Modeling for Requirements Engineering, pp. 457–484. MIT Press, Cambridge (2011)
8. Castro, J., Giorgini, P., Kolp, M., Mylopoulos, J.: Tropos: a requirements-driven methodology for agent-oriented software. In: Henderson-Sellers, B., Giorgini, P. (eds.) Agent-Oriented Methodologies. Idea Group (2005)
9. Dastani, M., Dix, J., Novák, P.: The second contest on multi-agent systems based on computational logic. In: Inoue, K., Satoh, K., Toni, F. (eds.) CLIMA VII. LNCS (LNAI), vol. 4371, pp. 266–283. Springer, Heidelberg (2007)
10. Dubois, E., Mayer, N., Rifaut, A.: Improving risk-based security analysis with i *. In: Yu, E., Giorgini, P., Maiden, N., Mylopoulos, J. (eds.) Social Modeling for Requirements Engineering. The MIT Press, Cambridge (2011)
11. Gluz, J.C., Vicari, R.M., Passerino, L.M.: An agent-based infrastructure for the support of learning objects life-cycle. In: Cerri, S.A., Clancey, W.J., Papadourakis, G., Panourgia, K. (eds.) ITS 2012. LNCS, vol. 7315, pp. 696–698. Springer, Heidelberg (2012)
12. Kolp, M., Wautelet, Y., Faulkner, S.: Sociocentric design of multiagent architectures. In: Yu, E., Giorgini, P., Maiden, N., Mylopoulos, J. (eds.) Social Modeling for Requirements Engineering. The MIT Press, Cambridge (2011)
13. Merriam-Webster: Merriam-Webster's Collegiate Dictionary, 11th edn. Merriam-Webster (2003)
14. OMG, Object Management Group: OMG Unified Modeling Language (OMG UML), Superstructure. Version 2.2. Object Management Group Standard (2009)
15. Polsani, P.R.: Use and abuse of reusable learning objects. J. Digit. Inf. 3, 1–10 (2003)
16. Popper, K.: The Logic of Scientific Discovery. Routledge, London (1992)
17. Silva, V., Noya, R.C., Lucena, C.J.P.: Using the UML 2.0 activity diagram to model agent plans and actions. In: Proceedings of 4th International Joint Conference on Autonomous Agents and Multiagent Systems (AAMAS). ACM, New York (2005)
18. Sklar, S., Richards, D.: The use of agents in human learning systems. In: Proceedings of 5th International Joint Conference on Autonomous Agents and Multiagent Systems (AAMAS), pp. 767–774 (2006)
19. Stoilescu, D.: Modalities of using learning objects for intelligent agents in learning. Interdisc. J. E-Learn. Learn. Objects 4, 49–64 (2008)
20. Vicari, R.M., Gluz, J.C.: An Intelligent Tutoring System (ITS) View on AOSE. Int. J. Agent-Oriented Softw. Eng. 1, 295–333 (2007)
21. Vicari, R.M., Jaques, P., Verdin, R.: Agent-Based Tutoring Systems by Cognitive and Affective Modeling. IGI Global, Hershey (2008)
22. Vygotsky, L.S.: Mind in Society: The Development of Higher Psychological Processes. Harvard University Press, Cambridge (1978)
23. Vygotsky, L.S.: Thought and Language. The M.I.T. Press, Cambridge (1986)
24. W3C: W3C Recommendation: OWL 2 Web Ontology Language: Structural Specification and Functional-Style Syntax, 2nd edn. W3C (2012)
25. Weiss, G.: Multiagent Systems, 2nd edn. MIT Press, Cambridge (2013)
26. Wiley, D.A.: Connecting learning objects to instructional design theory: a definition, a metaphor, and a taxonomy. In: The Instructional Use of Learning Objects, Association for Educational Communications and Technology, pp. 3–23 (2002)
27. Wongthongtham, P., Dillon, D., Dillon, T., Chang, E.: Use of UML 2.1 to model multi-agent systems based on a goal-driven software engineering ontology. In: 4th International Conference on Semantics, Knowledge and Grid (SKG 2008), pp. 428–432 (2008)
28. Wooldridge, M.: An Introduction to MultiAgent Systems. Wiley, Hoboken (2008)

29. Yu, E.: Modeling strategic relationships for process reengineering. In: Yu, E., Giorgini, P., Maiden, N., Mylopoulos, J. (eds.) Social Modeling for Requirements Engineering. The MIT Press, Cambridge (2011)
30. Yu, E., Giorgini, P., Maiden, N., Mylopoulos, J.: Social Modeling for Requirements Engineering. The MIT Press, Cambridge (2011)
31. Yu, E., Mylopoulos, J.: Towards modelling strategic actor relationships for information systems development - with examples from business process reengineering. In: Proceedings of the 4th Workshop on Information Technologies and Systems (1994)
32. Zabala, A.: La Practica Educativa. Como Enseñar. Editorial: IRIF, SL- Edit, Graó (1995)

New Moodle Blocks for Knowledge Management

Antonio Silva Sprock[1]([✉]) and Rosa Maria Vicari[2]

[1] Facultad de Ciencias, Escuela de Computación, Universidad Central de Venezuela,
Av. Los Ilustres, Los Chaguaramos, Caracas, Venezuela
antonio.silva@ciens.ucv.ve
[2] Centro Interdisciplinar de Tecnologias na Educação (CINTED), Universidade Federal do Rio
Grande do Sul (UFRGS), Porto Alegre, RS, Brazil
rosa@inf.ufrgs.br

Abstract. The paper shows the development of a module for Moodle, used to manage the knowledge involved in the process of teaching and learning, that includes Lessons Learned, Yellow Pages and FAQs, in addition to that we developed a Knowledge-Based Monitor which performs management of the students' activities. To evaluate the module developed, we used three validations, a usability test based on Nielsen's protocol for heuristic evaluation, the functionality test where 6 users completed 41 test cases, with satisfactory results, and finally the satisfaction survey, applied to 450 Moodle users.

Keywords: Knowledge management · Moodle · LMS · Knowledge based system

1 Context

The Learning Management Systems (LMS), also known as Course Management Systems (CMS), are web-based platforms that are used in e-learning. Their general functions are managing, monitoring and reporting the student interaction with the content, teacher and other students [1].

After the pioneer, Programmed Logic for Automated Teaching Operation (Plato) [2], hundreds of similar systems were introduced. An important milestone happened in 1997 when WebCT 1.0 was released and Blackboard was founded, because these two LMSs attracted millions of users. Moreover, after WebCT and Blackboard, the second milestone was the LMS Moodle (Modular Object Oriented Dynamic Learning Environment). It was introduced in 1998 and finally released in 2001 [3].

In [4], the author indicates that Moodle is the most common LMS with the largest community of developers around the world and versions in many languages [4]. Data obtained in March 2016, from official Moodle statics sites confirm the mentioned fact. It has been used by more than 83 million registered users, in more than 70 k registered sites around the world, and it is available in more than 100 languages [5].

Moodle and LMS have many advantages in the field of distance education, creating a student-teacher connection that results in an educational success [6]. The LMS can promote communication and interaction between students and teachers, and it is an useful tool that can contribute to the realization of an effective teaching and learning process.

© Springer International Publishing Switzerland 2016
F. Koch et al. (Eds.): SOCIALEDU 2015, CCIS 606, pp. 104–123, 2016.
DOI: 10.1007/978-3-319-39672-9_8

The Moodle functions are accomplished in modules: site management, user management, course management, task modules, chat room module, selecting module, forum module, logging module, test module, resource module, etc., which can be integrated and applied in a course design [7]. Moodle has also an ability of tracking the learner's progress that can be monitored by both teachers and learners [3].

In addition to that, students need to be self-disciplined, meeting deadlines and working steadily over the course. Thus, immature students who are not used to taking responsibility for their own learning can struggle even with well-designed courses [8].

In Moodle, these modules are offered to teachers separately, for its use in the different courses they structure. These tools are applied to the discretion of each teacher, without being aware of effectiveness of these resources, and if the tools are used they will lead to better results. Neither of them take into account the experience that can provide them other teachers and Moodle users.

In that sense, Herrera and Latapie [9] say that in the virtual classroom, it is not enough making available to the student the necessary resources to build their knowledge, it is important that it is truly usable, intuitive and ergonomic to transform the user experience more comfortable, enjoyable and significant.

In fact in [10] the author establishes that in terms of usability, Moodle is not easy to use for both students and teachers. He describes the feeling that the platform passes in the first entry is of bewilderment. Besides that, many tools and features make it loses important aspects, for example ease of use, comfort, and usability.

Using Moodle, teachers and students gain experience, that is tacit and individual knowledge, and all the track information about the use and the student's iteration with Moodle is loaded into its database, being a tacit knowledge too, until it is analyzed and used to improve the learning and teaching process in Moodle, and somehow, this knowledge is wasted currently.

The teachers and students experience is required to be used by others. It is necessary to know what knowledge teachers acquire using Moodle, who is who and management to track information and to monitor students in Moodle, namely working with knowledge. These aspects can help to improve the usability and accessibility in Moodle use.

Drucker [11] used the concept "knowledge worker" in his book "Landmarks of Tomorrow" in 1959. After this, many important authors have written about Knowledge Management (KM), as Steward [12], Nonaka and Kazuo [13], Nonaka and Takeuchi [14], Davenport [15], Prusak [16] and many others [17]. Simply, there are processes for making available the knowledge they need, to those in need, where they need them, as needed and when needed.

Then, it is necessary to structure and develop KM tools within Moodle, thus allowing better use of knowledge to harness the benefits of KM process, which the main purpose is to translate knowledge into action and this into results, and this goal is achieved when the tacit knowledge becomes explicit knowledge.

Some authors have written about the KM Techniques, [18] describes some of them, but we observe that some cannot be used with TICs, that is to say, they could not be integrated with Moodle, and we should consider only implementable techniques with Moodle.

Some papers report KM tools related with LMS. In [19] the authors present FindYourHelp, which is an additional module for Moodle that enables automatic identification of experts who make their contribution to discussion forums. This tool is based on applying text mining techniques as a supplementary analysis of students' participation in the existing environment. It allows the identification of who is who in the Moodle forum, a king of Yellow Pages.

Nagi [20] obtained the tracks registered in Moodle logs that were integrated with a Customer Relationship Management (CRM) application for four SME training courses offered as a part of SME Certificate program. The author's idea is to analyze the students' behavior in Moodle, to offer them alternatives and activities that can improve teaching and learning process.

Also, [21] presents an experience using Moodle wiki as an online didactic tool to develop KM processes in higher education. Throughout the study, 27 Egyptian students and 36 Italian students took part in online activities and developed interdisciplinary projects for the primary and preparatory stages while collaborating in a Wiki experience within Moodle platform.

Since now, this work has showed the development of the KM module in Moodle which includes: Lessons Learned by students and teachers, Yellow Pages of teachers, FAQs related to the use of the Moodle activities and a Knowledge-Based Monitor (KBM) which can check the student activities. These KM tools had already been conceptualized in previous work [22].

2   The Development

We developed four new tools to be inserted into Moodle, specifically we suggested: Yellow Pages, FAQs, Lessons Learned and the KBM. The KBM is a kind of a reactive agent which executes some rules for monitoring the students' activities in Moodle.

For the development of the Knowledge Management tools, we used the Scott Ambler Methodology [23], known as Agile Model Driven Development (AMDD) (Fig. 1).

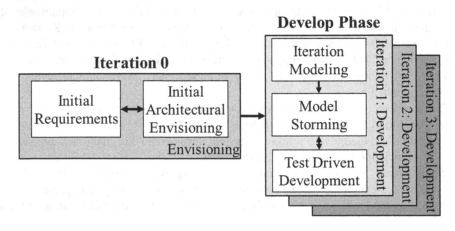

Fig. 1. Agile model driven development [23]

AMDD is iterative and incremental, divided in two phases: Iteration 0, which has two activities (Initial Requirements and Initial Architectural Envisioning) and Develop phase, which has three activities: Iteration Modeling, Model Storming and Test Driven Development.

2.1 Iteration 0

At the first phase, we developed the following three tasks:

1. The requirements analysis in which we determined the functional requirements of the KM tools that we implemented in Moodle. In this analysis, we applied knowledge acquisition techniques, specifically opening interviews and questionnaires, in which 3 teachers participated. They work in Database course, and they were very interested in this project.

   The functional requirements were defined for user roles (teacher, administrator, and student) and the KBM rules that will run with the Moodle activities (forum, assignment, quiz, questionnaire, wiki, FAQ, Lessons Learned and Yellow Pages). The Fig. 2 presents the use case diagram in which we show the functional requirements defined for each user role.

2. The definition of the KBM rules that will run with the Moodle activities (forum, assignment, questionnaire, quiz and wiki). These rules were structured for each activity, as shown below.

- Forum (KBM's rules for the Forum)
  - RF1: When adding or modifying a forum, send a SMS and email all students.
  - RF2: 24 h after creating a forum, send a SMS and email students who have not seen the forum.
  - RF3: 48 h after creating a forum, send a SMS and email students who have not participated in the forum.
  - RF4: Every 24 h send a SMS and email students who have not participated.
- Assignment (KBM's rules for the assignment)
  - RA1: When scheduling any activity, send a SMS and email all students.
  - RA2: 24 h before any scheduled activity, send a SMS and email all students.
  - RA3: 1 h before any scheduled activity, send a SMS and email all students.
- Questionnaire (KBM's rules for the questionnaire)
  - RQ1: When adding a questionnaire, send a SMS and email all students.
  - RQ2: 24 h after it created a questionnaire, send a SMS and email students who have not responded the questionnaire.
  - RQ3: 48 h after it created a questionnaire, send a SMS and email students who have not responded the questionnaire.
  - RQ4: When any student submits a questionnaire, send a SMS and email the teacher student data.
- Quiz (KBM's rules to the quiz)
  - RQZ1: When adding a quiz, send a SMS and email all students.

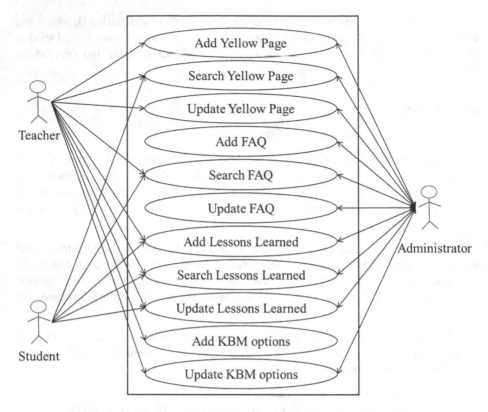

Fig. 2. Use case of the functional requirements defined for each user role

- RQZ2: 24 h after creating a quiz, send a SMS and email students who have not responded the quiz.
- RQZ3: 48 h after creating a quiz, send a SMS and email students who have not responded the quiz.
- RQZ4: when closing a quiz, send SMS and email the teacher with student data.
- Wiki (KBM's rules for the wiki)
  - RW1: When adding a Wiki, send a SMS and email all students and the teacher.
  - RW2: 24 h after creating a wiki, send a SMS and email students who have not participated in the wiki.
  - RW3: 48 h after creating a wiki, send a SMS and email students who have not participated in the wiki.
  - RW4: When any student participates in the wiki, send SMS and email the teacher with student data.

3. The analysis of the Moodle software (programing language, database), which we determined the software tools that we should use: we should use the Moodle's programming languages (PHP and HTML), CCS that facilitates the design of the HTML page, separating structure from presentation (colors, backgrounds, and letters), and JQuery which allows the fields validation during the execution, as well

as interaction with the user's server without page refresh. The Moodle's Database Management System is MySQL. We must modify and add some tables.

The other step in Iteration 0 is the Initial Architectural Envisioning, which we proposed two architectures, the first is the general architecture for the project, based on Model-View-Controller (MVC) in order to separate data, interface and control logic into three distinct components [24] (Fig. 3). The second architecture is related to KBM.

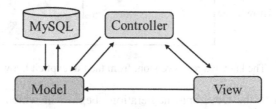

Fig. 3. MVC architecture and the used software tools

The other architecture corresponds to the KBM one. It was designed as a simple reactive element which compares inputs from environments with predetermined rules to determine actions to carry out. The Fig. 4 shows the KBM's architecture developed in this project.

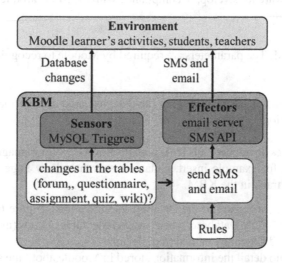

Fig. 4. The knowledge-based monitor

After completed the analysis and design of these architectures, we analyze how the new tools could help to manage knowledge involved in the process (Fig. 5).

The new tools can move the individual (tacit) knowledge to the group's domain, and transform it in explicit knowledge. Particularly, the FAQ begins in the group knowledge (teacher's group) and it flows to the student's group. In the next section, we explain the developed tools and the conversion of knowledge with these.

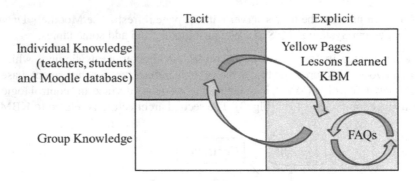

Fig. 5. The knowledge conversion: from tacit to explicit knowledge

After Iteration 0, the Development Iterations begins, in which we modified the Moodle Database and Interface, and included the new activities (FAQs, Lesson Learned, Yellow Pages and KBM) into Moodle.

2.2 Development Iterations

This phase activities were developed in two iterations. In the first interaction, we proposed the software to develop, in compliance with the MVC architecture (Fig. 3), as shown the following:

- Controlling
  - Control_KM: The parameters are required by Moodle to recognize the additional blocks.
- Model
  - Md_Sql: commands for managing the database, and also verifies all parameters for each action.
- View
  - All interfaces developed in HTML with PHP and CSS for managing the KM tools in Moodle, for example insert, update or search Yellow Page, FAQs, Lessons Learned or track in the KBM.

In this iteration, we also did the Database modifications. Figure 6 shows the new tables inserted in Moodle Database, where we include: tables FAQs (mdl_faqs), Yellow Pages (mdl_pa) and Lessons Learned (mdl_lecap).

We also got into detail the information stored in Moodle about the student activities (logs). Above we have said that Moodle has the ability of tracking the Moodle activities. The activities tracks are recorded in its Database, and the teacher or administrator could investigate it by functionality of auditing, using the Reports Module in the Administration Block (Fig. 7).

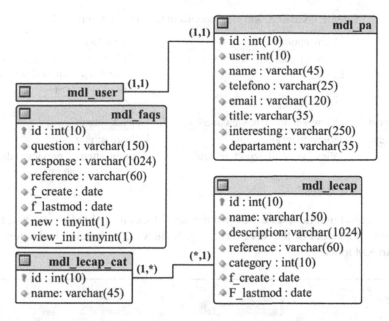

Fig. 6. New tables created in Moodle database

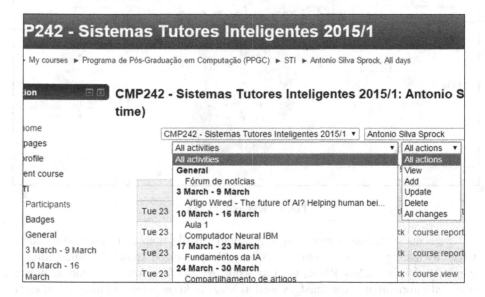

Fig. 7. Reports module in the Moodle administration block

The Reports Module displays many parameters as time, group, activity, IP address, user name, actions, even they can be used for filtering as shown in Table 1.

Table 1. Activities and view options in the Moodle report module

Activities	View options	Update options
Forum	View discussion, search, view forum	Add discussion, delete discussion, move discussion, add post, delete post, update post
Chat	View, report	Talk
Assignment	View, submission, view feedback	Upload, submit
Questionnaire	View, view all	Upload, submit
Quiz	View, view all, report, review	Attempt, attempt, preview, edit questions, delete attempts
Wiki	Views	Post

In the second iteration, we developed the new blocks into Moodle interface, related with View and Model of the MVC. The Fig. 8 shows the Moodle blocks developed, related to KM tools.

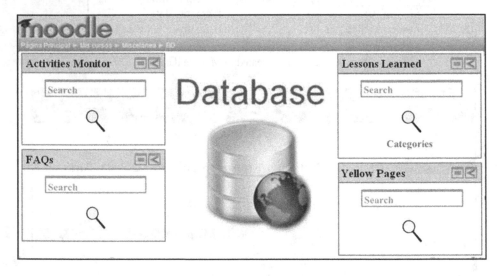

Fig. 8. KM tools blocks

In an educational environment, specifically in Moodle, users can "know who knows what" by finding and calling other teachers with specialized knowledge and skills. A good solution is Yellow Pages, used as white pages or personal directories, where personal information is collected, as well as areas of knowledge and interests of each person [25]. When the personal information is stored in the Yellow Pages, it becomes an explicit knowledge, because it goes from each teacher until a public and general domain (Fig. 9).

Then, when someone needs information about a topic, that person can search the list of the organization that knows him/her better and ask directly for help. These Yellow Pages are based on a technology that allows the user to find related information with

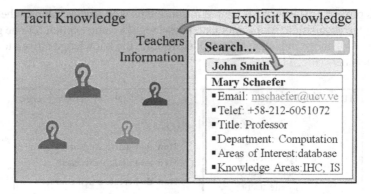

Fig. 9. The knowledge conversion with Yellow Pages

users of the KM system, and in turn, it serves to encourage dialogue with people within an institution. The yellow pages help to drive the dynamism process.

The second tool is Lessons Learned, they convey knowledge gained through experience, which are applicable to a task, decision or process so that when this knowledge is reused it impacts positively on results [26]. Lessons Learned helps to convert tacit knowledge (which is in the mind and comes from the experience of teachers and students, gained using Moodle) in explicit knowledge (Fig. 10).

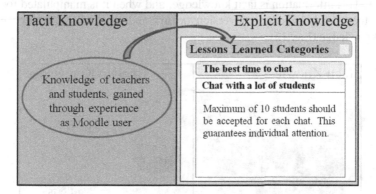

Fig. 10. The knowledge conversion with Lesson Learned

Teachers to implement a course in Moodle, effectively and efficiently, must have a comprehensive and detailed knowledge about important aspects of the activities and the platform for development course.

The other tool is FAQs. The purpose of them is to provide a tool that helps to find FAQs documents related for a query, stored in a database to help teachers in solving problems and questions that appear frequently [27].

According to [27], FAQs include the most common questions on a particular topic, by providing knowledge and strategies to assist them in finding a solution to the problem they are facing.

In this project, FAQs were structured in consensus with teachers during the process of knowledge acquisition. At this moment, knowledge became explicit for one group of teachers and when we implemented FAQ in Moodle, the knowledge moved to a larger group of teachers (Fig. 11).

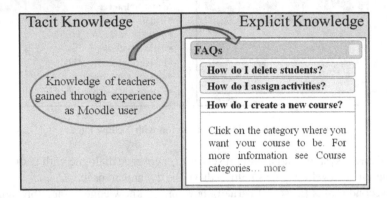

Fig. 11. The knowledge conversion with FAQs

The last developed tool is the KBM. This is composed of PHP code and Database Triggers for managing the Moodle Logs. This Log stores the student activities, indicated in Table 1. This information is tacit knowledge, and when it is manipulated for student tracking, then the knowledge conversion occurs and the tacit knowledge becomes explicit knowledge (Fig. 12).

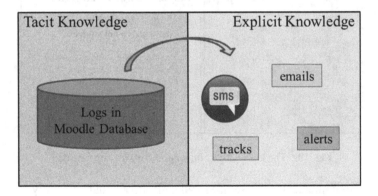

Fig. 12. The knowledge conversion with the KBM

The KBM options are shown in Fig. 13, where you can include all possible options for a new track, according to the rules of KBM indicated previously.

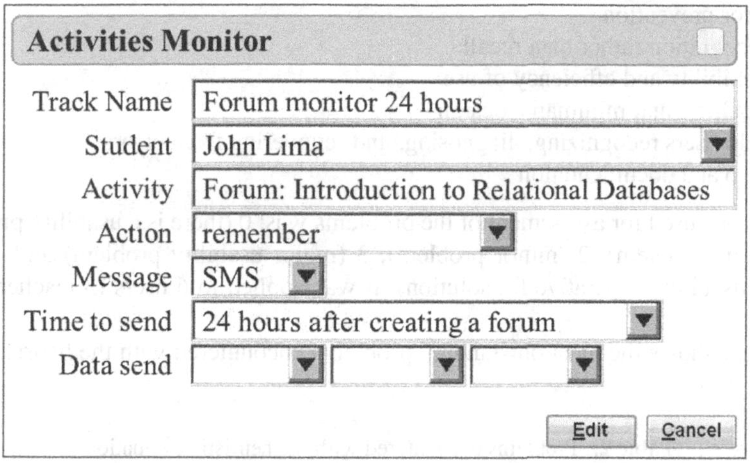

Fig. 13. KBM options

3 Validation

For the validation process of the blocks incorporated in Moodle, we did three types of validation. The first was the usability validation, the second was the functional validation and the third one was a satisfaction survey.

3.1 Usability Validation

ISO defines usability as the ability of a product to be used by specific users to achieve specific goals with effectiveness, efficiency and satisfaction in a specific context of use [28]. This definition is very enlightening due to the following aspects: effectiveness, efficiency and satisfaction.

One of the usability evaluation systems of "inspection" type is the heuristic evaluation, in which some evaluators examine the interface, following the usability principles (heuristics). The review is done individually and must assume the role of a user. Until the evaluation is not completely performed, you are not allowed to communicate the results to evaluators [29].

Some authors have worked on the evaluation called user-centered [30–33]. In that sense, Mari-Carmen Marcos [29] indicates that Nielsen's proposal [31] is one of the most used one.

In the usability validation, we did the test that consisted of analyzing the conformity of the interface with recognized usability principles (heuristics) and correspond to Jakob Nielsen's 10 general principles for interaction design [31]:

(1) Visibility of system status
(2) Match between system and the real world
(3) User control and freedom
(4) Consistency and standards

(5) Error prevention
(6) Recognition rather than recall
(7) Flexibility and efficiency of use
(8) Aesthetic and minimalist design
(9) Help users recognizing, diagnosing, and recovering from errors
(10) Help and documentation

The scale used for assessment of the problems was: 0 (there is a usability problem), 1 (cosmetic problem), 2 (minor problem), 3 (major usability problem) and 4 (catastrophic usability imperative fix solution). It was applied to 6 users (3 teachers and 3 students).

Table 2 shows the most outstanding problems encountered with the heuristic evaluation.

Table 2. Problems encountered with the heuristic evaluation

Problem	Heuristic	Assessment	Solution
The categories of the Lessons Learned have not been sorted	H1	4	Organize content
Some Yellow Pages data are not mandatory	H4	5	All fields are required
Not showing the shortcuts in the KBM options	H7	4	Include shortcuts in each attribute and each option

The test had positive opinions about usability. It is necessary to note that the questionnaire sought opinions related to investigate usability issues reported by Nielsen [31], therefore to obtain a greater number of favorable responses, it means that the application was approved in the usability test.

3.2 Functional Validation

The second validation consisted of forty-one (41) cases of evaluation, covering fully all functional levels of the new blocks for the KM tools and the KBM. The importance of this test is to validate the proper functioning into Moodle, of each and every one of the functions defined, that it is to say if it meets all the functional requirements previously defined. If any test fails, the related function should be repaired.

6 users (3 teachers and 3 students) participated in these tests. They entered in the system as teacher, administrator and student. The tests, as it was indicated previously, related each functional requirement defined and the KBM Rules defined in each Moodle activity.

The new Moodle blocks were tested in the Database course, so three teachers belong to the Database area, and three students represent a sample of twelve students enrolled in the course. It is a first evaluation which will be extended to a larger sample in the future.

We used the Likert scales [34] with the typical format of five levels of responses (5. strongly agree, 4. agree, 3. neither agree nor disagree, 2. disagree and 1. strongly disagree).

Then we show the questions and the percentages of responses given to each question, by the group from 6 users.

- Questions of functional requirements:
    (1) TFR1: Search Yellow Pages is successfully?: 100 % strongly agree.
    (2) TFR1: Search FAQs is successfully?: 100 % strongly agree.
    (3) TFR1: Search Lessons Learned is successfully?: 83.33 % strongly agree and 16.66 % agree.
    (4) TFR2: Adding Yellow Pages is successfully?: 100 % strongly agree.
    (5) TFR2: Adding Lessons Learned is successfully?: 100 % strongly agree.
    (6) TFR3: Update Yellow Page attributes is successfully?: 100 % strongly agree.
    (7) TFR4: Update Lessons Learned is successfully?: 100 % strongly agree.
    (8) TFR5: Update KBM options is successfully?: 100 % strongly agree.
    (9) AFR1: Search Yellow Pages is successfully?: 83.33 % strongly agree and 16.66 % agree.
    (10) AFR1: Search FAQs is successfully?: 100 % strongly agree.
    (11) AFR1: Search Lessons Learned is successfully?: 100 % strongly agree.
    (12) AFR2: Adding Yellow Pages is successfully?: 83.33 % strongly agree and 16.66 % agree.
    (13) AFR2: Adding FAQs is successfully?: 100 % strongly agree.
    (14) AFR2: Adding Lessons Learned is successfully?: 83.33 % strongly agree and 16.66 % agree.
    (15) AFR3: Update Yellow Pages attributes is successfully?: 100 % strongly agree.
    (16) AFR4: Update Lessons Learned is successfully?: 83.33 % strongly agree and 16.66 % agree.
    (17) AFR5: Update KBM options is successfully?: 100 % strongly agree.
    (18) SFR1: Search Yellow Pages is successfully?: 100 % strongly agree.
    (19) SFR1: Search FAQs is successfully?: 83.33 % strongly agree and 16.66 % agree.
    (20) SFR1: Search Lessons Learned is successfully?: 100 % strongly agree.
    (21) SFR2: Adding Lessons Learned is successfully?: 100 % strongly agree.
    (22) SFR3: Update Lessons Learned is successfully?: 83.33 % strongly agree and 16.66 % agree.
- Questions of KBM Rules:
    (23) RF1: When adding or modifying a forum, should the system send a SMS and email all students?: 100 % strongly agree.
    (24) RF2: 24 h after creating a forum, should the system send a SMS and email all students who have not seen the forum?: 100 % strongly agree.
    (25) RF3: 48 h after creating a forum, should the system send a SMS and email students who have not participated in the forum?: 83.33 % strongly agree and 16.66 % agree.
    (26) RF4: Every 24 h, should the system send a SMS and email students who have not participated in the forum?: 83.33 % strongly agree and 16.66 % agree.

(27) RA1: When scheduling any activity, should the system send a SMS and email all students?: 83.33 % strongly agree and 16.66 % agree.

(28) RA2: 24 h before any scheduling activity, should the system send a SMS and email all students?: 83.33 % strongly agree and 16.66 % agree.

(29) RA3: 1 h prior to any scheduled activity, should the system send a SMS and email all students, is it successfully?: 66.66 % strongly agree and 33.33 % agree.

(30) RQ1: By adding a questionnaire, should the system send a SMS and email all students?: 83.33 % strongly agree and 16.66 % agree.

(31) RQ2: 24 h after creating a questionnaire, should the system send a SMS and email students who have not responded to the questionnaire?: 100 % strongly agree.

(32) RQ3: 48 h after creating a questionnaire, should the system send a SMS and email students who have not responded to the questionnaire?: 100 % strongly agree.

(33) RQ4: When performing submits a questionnaire, should the system send a SMS and email a student data to the teacher?: 83.33 % strongly agree and 16.66 % agree.

(34) RQZ1: To add a quiz, should the system send a SMS and email all students?: 100 % strongly agree.

(35) RQZ2: 24 h after creating a quiz, should the system send a SMS and email students who have not responded the quiz?: 83.33 % strongly agree and 16.66 % agree.

(36) RQZ3: 48 h after creating a quiz, should the system send a SMS and email students who have not responded the quiz?: 100 % strongly agree.

(37) RQZ4: When closing a quiz, should the system send a SMS and email the teacher with student data?: 100 % strongly agree.

(38) RW1: To add a Wiki, should the system send a SMS and email all students and the teacher?: 83.33 % strongly agree and 16.66 % agree.

(39) RW2: 24 h after creating a wiki, should the system send a SMS and email students who have not participated?: 100 % strongly agree.

(40) RW3: 48 h after creating a wiki, should the system send a SMS and email students who have not participated in the wiki?: 66.66 % strongly agree and 33.33 % agree.

(41) RW4: When making a wiki post, should the system send a SMS and email the student data to the teacher?: 100 % strongly agree.

20 (48.78 %) of the cases had responses with 6 users strongly agree, 12 (29.26 %) of the cases had 5 users strongly agree and 1 user agree responses and finally 9 (21.95 %) of the cases had 4 users strongly agree and 1 users agree responses. The options "neither agree nor disagree", "disagree" and "strongly disagree" were not used (Fig. 14). This result allows the validation of the system functionally, because 100 % of the answers were strongly agree or agree.

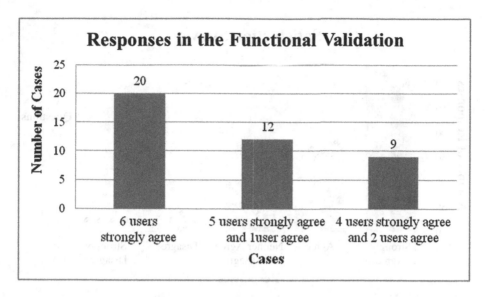

Fig. 14. Responses of the functional validation

3.3 Satisfaction Survey

The third and last validation was a satisfaction survey applied to 40 professors and 400 students at the Universidad Central de Venezuela. The 450 evaluators were being Moodle users at the university. The survey had the following 4 questions:

(1) When do you use the new Moodle blocks, is it intuitively performed?
(2) The knowledge management is the processes of making available the knowledge they need, to those in need, where they need them, as needed and when needed. According to this statement, do the new Moodle blocks satisfy the expectations of knowledge management?
(3) The usability is the ability of a product to be used by specific users to achieve specific goals with effectiveness, efficiency and satisfaction in a specific context of use. According to this statement, are the interfaces developed usable?
(4) Would you recommend the system developed to colleagues and other students?

The responses associated to a Likert scale [34] with five levels of responses (5. strongly agree, 4. agree, 3. neither agree nor disagree, 2. disagree and 1. strongly disagree) (Fig. 15).

In question 1: When do you use the new Moodle blocks, is it intuitively performed?, 59.33 % of the responses were "strongly agree" and 32.45 % were "agree", this represents 91.78 % of users that think that it is performed intuitively. 8.22 % of the responses were "neither agree nor disagree".

In question 2: Do the new Moodle blocks satisfy the expectations of knowledge management?, 66.44 % of the responses were "strongly agree" and 28 % were "agree", this represents the 94.44 % of users that think that the new Moodle blocks satisfy the

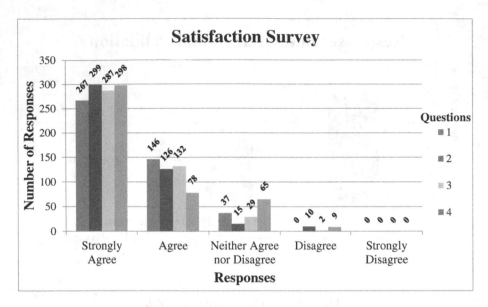

Fig. 15. Satisfaction survey responses

expectations of knowledge management. 3.33 % of the responses were "neither agree nor disagree", and 2.22 % were "disagree".

In question 3: Are the interfaces developed usable?, the answers were similar, 63.78 % of the responses were "strongly agree" and 29.33 % were "agree", this represents the 93.11 % of users that think that the developed interfaces are usable. 6.44 % of the responses were "neither agree nor disagree" and only 0.44 % of the responses were "disagree".

In question 4: Would you recommend the system developed to colleagues and other students?, 66.22 % of the responses were "strongly agree" to recommend it, 17.33 % were "agree", 14.44 % were "neither agree nor disagree", and finally 2 % of the respondents disagree about this. 83.55 % of them would recommend it.

All questions had similar responses. The "strongly agree" option had the highest responses, the second most chosen option was "agree" and third most chosen option "neither agree nor disagree". The option "disagree" was the less answered, and the option "strongly disagree" did not appear in any response.

4   Conclusions

The use of LMS has grown in education institutions to offer new alternatives in the teaching and learning process, allowing us to offer e-learning courses, or supporting in a system of classroom education. However, it is always looking for new resources or services that may be offered, for that reason four tools of knowledge management were developed: Yellow Pages, Lessons Learned, FAQs and a Knowledge-Based Monitor, which were integrated into Moodle LMS. Until the completion of this work it was possible to successfully develop a set of tools, to provide tangible support for teachers and students that make this platform a vital tool in the teaching and learning process.

The developed tools have the following advantages: they are free, not limited to any specific educational area, they enable knowledge management, they ensure that data and experiences of other teachers and students are not wasted and they offer continuing improvements in materials and courses.

For the validation of the developed tools, we did three processes, the usability validation, the functional validation and the satisfaction survey. We obtained satisfactory results on these, and this allowed the validation of: usability, functionality and satisfaction.

As future works, we suggest testing in some others courses implemented, considering control groups and experimentation in order to evaluate the management of knowledge and its impact on real cases. Likewise, it is recommended as a possible extension of this work, the implementation of a module that allows teachers subscribing to specific topics of interest, and which in turn they are notified by sending email when there are new entries.

Similarly, in the future it is important that the learning and teaching environment could be an intelligent environment based on semantic web which can find and recommend significant contents to the students.

In addition to that, the KBM developed is merely reactive and this approach did not incorporate intelligence. We could add some automatic learning or Bayesian models in the KBM in order to analyze some user behaviors and to recommend different strategies among yellow pages, Lessons learned and FAQ.

Finally, the development will be released within the Moodle development community to be incorporated in new versions.

References

1. Moreno, J., Ovalle, D., Vicari, R.: Hacia una Taxonomía en la Educación Asistida por Computador. Educación en Ingeniería. Asociación Colombiana de Facultades de Ingeniería 5(9), 27–36 (2010)
2. Stapic, Z., Orehovacki, T., Danic, M.: Determination of optimal security settings for LMS Moodle. In: 31st MIPRO International Convention on Information Systems Security, vol. 5, pp. 84–89 Opatija (2008)
3. Kumar, S., Gankotiya, A., Dutta, K.: A comparative study of MOODLE and other e-learning systems. In: 3rd International Conference on Electronics Computer Technology, pp. 414–418. IEEE, Kanyakumari (2011)
4. Flores, N.V.: Plataforma Web Moodle para su aplicación en el proceso de enseñanza-aprendizaje (2007). http://labsys.frc.utn.edu.ar/pdf/paper_proyecto_Moodle.pdf
5. Moodle Statistics, 27 February 2016. https://moodle.net/stats/?lang=es
6. Díaz, S.: Introducción a las Plataformas Virtuales en la Enseñanza (2009). http://www2.fe.ccoo.es/andalucia/docu/p5sd4920.pdf
7. Jin, S.: Design of an online learning platform with Moodle. In: 7th International Conference on Computer Science and Education (ICCSE 2012), pp. 1710–1714. IEEE Press, Melbourne, Australia (2012)

8. Simsek, A.: Interview with tony bates on the aspects and prospects of online learning. Contemp. Educ. Technol **2**(1), 88–94 (2011). Online Submission

9. Herrera, M., Latapie, I.: Diseñando para la educación (2010). http://www.nosolousabilidad.com/articulos/diseno_educacion.htm

10. Flores, N.V.: Plataforma Web Moodle para su aplicación en el proceso de enseñanza-aprendizaje (2007). http://labsys.frc.utn.edu.ar/pdf/paper_proyecto_Moodle.pdf

11. Drucker, P.: Landmarks of Tomorrow. Harper and Row, New York (1959)

12. Stewart, T.: Intellectual Capital: The New Wealth of Organizations. Doubleday, New York (1997)

13. Nonaka, I., Kazuo, I.: Knowledge Creation and Management. Oxford University Press, New York (2007)

14. Nonaka, I., Takeuchi, H.: Knowledge-Creating Company. Oxford University Press, Oxford, New York (1995)

15. Davenport, T.: Knowledge management case study: knowledge management at Microsoft. University of Texas, McCombs School of Business, Austin, TX (1997). http://www.bus.utexas.edu/kman/microsoft.htm

16. Prusak, L.: Where did knowledge management come from? IBM Syst. J. **40**(4), 1002–1007 (2001). http://www.research.ibm.com/journal/sj/404/prusak.html

17. Liberona, D.: Revisión de investigación de Gestión del Conocimiento (2012). SSRN 1986195

18. Disterer, G.: Management of project knowledge and experiences. J. Knowl. Manag. **6**(5), 512–520 (2002)

19. Santos, M.L., Salvador, L.N., Cruces, D.: FindYourHelp: an expert finder module on Virtual Learning Environments. Informática na Educação: teoria & prática **14**(2), 95–112. Universidad Federal do Rio Grande do Sul, Brasil (2011). http://seer.ufrgs.br/index.php/InfEducTeoriaPratica/article/view/14156/16842

20. Nagi, K.: Use of moodle reports for knowledge management, planning and eTraining in SMEs. In: 4th IEEE International Conference on Management of Innovation and Technology (ICMIT 2008), pp. 946–950, Bangkok (2008). http://ieeexplore.ieee.org/stamp/stamp.jsp?tp=&arnumber=4654494

21. Biasuttia, M., EL-Deghaidy, H.: Using Wiki in teacher education: impact on knowledge management processes and student satisfaction. Comput. Educ. **59**(3), 861–872 (2012)

22. Silva Sprock, A., Ponce Gallegos, J., Meneses Hernández, J.: Gestionando el Conocimiento en Moodle. In: VIII Conferencia Latinoamericana de Objetos de Aprendizaje y Tecnologías para el Aprendizaje (LACLO 2013), pp. 1–12. Universidad Austral de Chile, Valdivia, Chile (2013). http://www.laclo.org/papers/index.php/laclo/article/view/84/78

23. Ambler, S.: Agile Modeling: Effective Practices for Extreme Programming and the Unified Process (2002). http://www.agilemodeling.com/essays/introductionToAM.htm

24. Lago, R.: Patrones de diseño de software. Patrón "Modelo-Vista-Contralador" (2007). http://www.proactiva-calidad.com/java/patrones/mvc.html

25. Navarro, S.: Gestión del conocimiento. Una práctica para mejorar la eficiencia de la empresa actual (2006). http://www.iit.upcomillas.es/pfc/resumenes/42ba671529b08.pdf

26. Mazoni, G.M.: Modelo para la gestión del conocimiento y la experiencia integrada a las prácticas y procesos de desarrollo de software (2010). http://www.ort.edu.uy/fi/pdf/tesismatturro2010.pdf

27. Bortolon, A., Wangenheim, C.G., Domingos, M.: Uma Abordagem Híbrida para o Gerenciamento de Documentos FAQ Em Português (2001). http://www.ensode.net/pdf-crack.jsf;jsessionid=ee31c8d179940baeb29d1eab6611

28. ISO 9241: Ergonomic Requirements for Office Work with Visual Display Terminals. International Organization for Standardization, Géneve (1997)

29. Marcos, M., Mesa, B., Ortega, M., Benmakhlouf, H., Dwelle, P., Hernández, P., Pérez, J., Renau, I., Serván, I., Davradou, E., López, F., Malvar, P., Mayor, A., Morales, A.: Evaluación de la usabilidad en sistemas de información terminológicos Hipertext.net. **4** (2006). http://www.hipertext.net
30. Simpson, H.: Design of User-Friendly Programs for Small Computers. McGraw-Hill, New York (1985)
31. Nielsen, J.: Heuristic evaluation. In: Nielsen, J., Mack, R.L. (eds.) Usability Inspection Methods. Wiley, New York (1994)
32. Rogers, Y., Preece, J., Sharp, H.: Interaction Design: Beyond Human-Computer Interaction. Wiley, New York (2011)
33. Shneiderman, B.: Designing the User Interface, 3rd edn. Addison-Wesley, Reading, MA (1997)
34. Likert, R.A.: Technique for the Measurement of Attitudes. Archives of Psychology. Columbia University Press, New York (1931)

Experimental Evaluation on Machine Learning Techniques for Human Activities Recognition in Digital Education Context

Gabriel Leitão[1]([✉]), Juan Colonna[1], Erick Ribeiro[1], Raimundo Barreto[1], Thierry-Yves Araujo[1], Anny Martins[1], Andrew Koster[2], and Fernando Koch[2]

[1] Institute of Computing, Federal University of Amazonas (UFAM), Manaus, Brazil
{gabriel.leitao,juancolonna,err,rbarreto}@icomp.ufam.edu.br
[2] Samsung Research Institute, Campinas, SP, France
{andrew.k,fernando.koch}@samsung.com
http://www.icomp.ufam.edu.br

Abstract. This paper describes an experimental evaluation of the main machine learning supervised techniques to be used for the human activities recognition in the context of technological education using data collected from smartphones sensors. The overall goal is to use the recognition of activities to identify students with attention deficit or hyperactivity problems, by recognizing three activities: walking, standing and sitting. Hence, this work focuses on developing activities recognition method of the students. The methodology consists in: collecting data where the user explicitly states what activity he/she is doing; applying various techniques to automatically recognize the activities; and measuring the degree of accuracy of each technique. The results shows that techniques such as Bayesian inference and SVM (Support Vector Machine) have smaller accuracy than techniques based on decision tree and kNN (k-nearest neighbors). Furthermore, the techniques based on decision trees have a constant computational cost, while the kNN depends on the number of samples.

Keywords: HAR · Human activities recognition · Machine learning · Digital education

1 Introduction

The context of this paper is within Samsung Research Brazil's Digital Education initiative, aimed at investigating new models of learning technology models, instrumentation of the learning environment, assessment of educational performance, intelligent recommendation, and tools for supporting planning activities in the classroom, all with the main aim to improve the education quality. In this context, we want to promote the correlation between educational tools with student behavior to infer more appropriate learning styles parameters.

© Springer International Publishing Switzerland 2016
F. Koch et al. (Eds.): SOCIALEDU 2015, CCIS 606, pp. 124–139, 2016.
DOI: 10.1007/978-3-319-39672-9_9

An area that is gaining a lot of terrain in the current research is the Human Behavior Computational Analysis, which usually investigates computational methods for multimodal detection and modeling to better capture, analyze and understand qualitative, social and emotional aspects of human behavior.

In this case, it is possible to analyze and to extract information from gestures, touch, movement, body language and even posture using sensors. Starting from these sensor signals, we can infer new information which we call "honest signals" [1]; i.e. people emit their activities and intentions, without even being aware of it. For example, a person who is walking from one side of the room to the other may be sending a signal, often without realizing it, that he/she is anxious or apprehensive. To capture the honest signals we can adopt several kinds of sensors.

In this paper, we are particularly interested in the use of smartphones because they have several different kinds of sensors (among others, an accelerometer, gyroscope, GPS, direction, and lighting sensor) and some of them can be used to make such recognition at a relatively low cost, mainly because we consider that the vast majority of students already have one. The human behavior analysis can be very useful in recognition of activities that help the education area, where you can find evidence of, for example, attention deficit, hyperactivity, sleeping, level of engagement, task orderliness and even emotional involvement level.

We evaluated experimentally the main techniques to automatically recognize some human activities (walking, standing and sitting) in applications in technological education. The adopted metrics were F-score, accuracy and computational cost. Although there are several methods that can be used for the recognition of human activities, in this paper we focused on machine learning techniques, which are techniques that give computers the ability to learn without being explicitly programmed. Learning can be supervised or unsupervised. However, in this paper we will only take into account supervised approach, which are techniques that need to be trained before making the classifications and recognitions.

The rest of the paper is organized as follows. Section 2 presents the main concepts and definitions necessary for the understanding of the paper. Section 3 summarizes the main related work, and Sect. 4 describes the proposed methodology. Section 5 details the experimental results, and Sect. 6 describes the app implemented. Finally, the Sect. 7 presents the concluding remarks and future directions of this research.

2   Background

Mobile devices are increasingly integrated into the daily lives of people, helping them in several types of activities. More recent devices have a set of sensors capable of monitoring environmental variables (atmospheric pressure, ultraviolet rays, temperature), biological (heartbeat), physical (speed, acceleration, geospatial coordinates), and others. Among these devices, the smartphones are the most popular because they run various tasks, are easy to carry, to use and have affordable cost.

The focus of this paper is the recognition of human activities in technological education context. As we are considering that most students carry a smartphone on their person, and this is the device on which we have concentrated our initial approach. Thus, we will use the Linear Acceleration sensors, Gyroscope and Orientation, available in smartphones, to measure movement of the device and classify some activities performed by the students.

2.1 Sensors

Linear Acceleration. The linear acceleration sensor measures the acceleration event of a smartphone along three predefined axes (Fig. 1(a)). This measurement results in three spatial vectors (x, y, z - motion) and one time vector i, such that: $Acc_i =< x_i, y_i, z_i >, i = (1, 2, 3, ...)$. This sensor measures acceleration while excluding the effect gravity [2].

The data obtained through this sensor allows us to infer the physical motion of its holder. Thus, if someone is walking and, stops suddenly, there is a change in the amplitude and frequency of the signal from the sensor axis (Fig. 2). This information is very relevant to the recognition of some human activities [3].

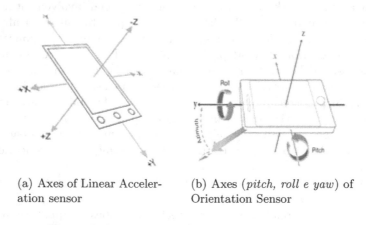

(a) Axes of Linear Acceleration sensor

(b) Axes (*pitch, roll e yaw*) of Orientation Sensor

Fig. 1. Reference axes of different types of sensors.

Gyroscope. The Gyroscope measures the rotational rate of smartphone from the motion of the axes of rotation (x), pitch (y) and direction(z). The data are given in rad/s (*radians per second*) and assist applications for navigation and games. In research into recognizing human activities the Gyroscope can, together with the Accelerometer, assist in detection of the mobile orientation and improve accuracy in human activities classification [3].

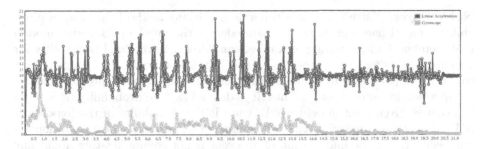

Fig. 2. Signs from Linear Acceleration and Gyroscope

Figure 2 shows the modules of linear acceleration and gyroscope in the same time interval. We can verify that between 0 and 14.0 there is more oscillation in the waveform behavior than between 14.0 and 21.0.

Orientation. The orientation sensor provides the smartphone position relative to magnetic north of earth using the rotation in the vertical, transverse and longitudinal axes to calculate the angles generated by movements pitch, roll and yaw (or azimuth) showed in Fig. 1(b). The angles generated by this sensor are widely used in the classification of activities like walking, running, sitting or standinbehrg up because there are angular variations in motions calculated by this sensor.

2.2   Machine Learning

There are several approaches to classify human activities and many of them use machine learning techniques which allow the computer, from a set of features, to "learn" and "classify" what activity is happening. In this paper, we choose to use supervised methods, i.e., those having both training and test phases [4]. The training is to "teach" the algorithm what information is relevant in a set of features and what class they must be associated with [4]. In our work, the feature set is coming from smartphone sensors. That is, each sensor contributes with one or more features that helps the classification algorithm to recognize a particular activity.

k-Nearest Neighbor (kNN). According to Kaghyan and Hakob [5], K-NN is a non-parametric learning algorithm that is popular for supervised pattern recognition. The main concept of this algorithm is to classify a new object from attributes and training samples. It uses classification using the neighborhood (the "k" nearest neighbors in the feature space) to predict the value of the instance in question. During the training, it is important to feed the algorithm with the correct information.

Naive Bayes. Naive Bayes is a supervised learning method that uses a probabilistic model based on previous knowledge of the problem (Bayesian model) that, combined with training examples, can determine the final probability for a sample belonging to any group [6]. Naive Bayes assumes that, given a set that contains groups divided by values and attributes, it is possible to predict in which group a new instance belongs. Thus, it is defined as "the probability of A given B", that is, given a set of evidence B, what is the probability of the hypothesis A [7]. It is called "naive" because it assumes that attributes are conditionally independent, i.e., the information of an event is not communicating about any other (which does not happen in the most of practical problems).

SVM - Support Vector Machine. SVM is a technique based on Statistical Learning Theory [8], where they establish a number of principles to be followed in obtaining classifiers with good generalization, and the ability to correctly predict the class of new data from the same domain in which the learning occurs. The basic idea of this method is to build a decision surface (hyperplane) in the feature space that best separates the training samples of the different classes. To perform this task, this method uses predicting variables called attributes. When an attribute is used in constructing the hyperplane, it is called a "feature", and the set of features selected to describe a classification is named a "vector". The vectors nearby the hyperplane are the support vectors. In practice, the goal of an SVM is to find a linear hyperplane (decision limit) with a high level of generalization for the examples provided as input in the classification process.

C4.5. Decisions trees are simple representation of knowledge and have been used to implement classification algorithms. Thus, decision trees are effective methods of supervised learning [9]. In a decision tree each *leaf* node is a decision, i.e., a class and each *branch* represents a test [10].

In 1979, Quinlan [11] introduced one algorithm for training a decision tree, ID3, and in 1993, he presented the C4.5 algorithm as an improvement of the first [12]. His method uses *Shannon Entropy* (probability distribution) to calculate the *Information Gain* and *Gain Ratio*, and measure the degree of mixing of the classes. After this, it can rank the attributes and build the decision tree [10].

PART. PART is an algorithm for creating a set of classification rules that are learned one by one without requiring a global optimization procedure [13]. The inference of the rules is generated repeatedly by partial decision trees. Thus, this method combines two main paradigms: "decision trees" and "divide and conquer". Moreover, this method avoids post-processing (tree pruning), increasing the speed of training compared to C4.5, for instance. The main advantages of PART compared to other techniques applied to our domain are: the best performance in the classification rate (Sect. 5) and the simplicity of the generated rules.

For our application, each generated rule is $r : (condition) \rightarrow$ "*Activity*", and the final set of all rules is $R = \{r_1, r_2, \cdots, r_n\}$. The "conditions" are built from feature vector presented in Sect. 4. Thus, if all attributes of an instance satisfies the conditions of the rule (e.g. r_x), then, the rule "covers" the instance and the result is given by the "Activity" label. For example, given the rule:

$$r_1 : \parallel gyro_{s1} \parallel > 0.79 \ \& \parallel acc_{s1} \parallel < 2.24 \ \& \parallel gyro_{std} \parallel \leq 2.03 \ \&$$
$$\parallel acc_{s1} \parallel > 2.59 \ \& \ roll_{s1} \leq 20.19 \rightarrow walking$$

If all conditions of r_1 are satisfied, then we can infer that the person is walking. In other case, if at least one condition is not satisfied, then the remaining rules of R must to be tested. As we can see, the simplicity of the rules allows them to be embedded in the smartphone with a low cost of memory, besides being an updatable model that will allow us to include a larger set of activities in the future.

3   Related Works

Accelerometers and other sensors have been widely used in human activity recognition. The processing of data from sensors and classification of a particular activity depends on the approach used. Thus, Zhang et al. [14] used a hierarchical model to classify six everyday activities: walking, posture transition, gentle motion, standing, sitting and lying. The approach of this work uses Kalman filters to reduce the bias introduced by noise from the sensor, and subsequently utilizes the SVM classifier to discriminate whether the activity is "motionless" or "motion", and then, from the inside of one of these classes, to select one of the six target activities. According to the authors, this approach has obtained 82.8 % accuracy for the classification of six activities.

Khan et al. [15] used an approach with different types of coefficients associated with Artificial Neural Networks to classify four activities: lying down, sitting, walking and running. The technique proposed achieves approximately 99 % accuracy in the activities classification.

In addition to the accelerometer, Tapia et al. [16] proposed the use of heartbeat sensor to increase the accuracy in classification. A total of three major classes (posture, activities with multiple intensities, other activities) have been uses and, inside of each one, subclasses, such as: lying down, walking, running, among other. They used classifiers based on Naive Bayes and decision trees (C4.5 DT), in conjunction with other processes involving calculations of distances of the axes, variance, and peaks in FFT.

Long et al. [17] classified five activities: walking, running, cycling, driving and sports. This study compared a method of Bayesian classification (Naive Bayes) with another approach based on decision trees (CAR). *Principal Component Analysis (PCA)* was used for the correlation between the features and to reduce the characteristic dimension of the vector. The classifier based on the decision tree obtained 72.8 % accuracy, while Naive Bayes obtained 71,5 % accuracy (without PCA) and 72,5 % (with PCA), respectively. It was noticed that main trouble was the ambiguity of the features related to activities such as walking, running and sports.

Koster et al. [18] proposed a highly adaptive context inference method called Big Context. The goal is to recognize patterns in data and make a composition with different contexts, but without a previous understanding of these patterns or the analysis rules. In general, they use probabilistic recognition of activities, which analyzes the signals and its impact on a given sequence of observations, besides the modeling and the classification of semantic context, which provides support to reasoning through analysis of context and semantic rules. As proof of concept, the authors presented a prototype of an application to find a parking spot and to help the user to find where parked his car. This work is interesting because it allows the adjustment of recognizers to deal with unexpected situations.

Zhang et al. [14], Khan et al. [15] present works that require a high processing power because they use techniques such as SVM and Artificial Neural Networks, respectively. Tapia et al. [16], beyond accelerometer, use an approach with FFT and heartbeat sensor. Long et al. [17] reduce the dimensionality using PCA, but this implies in ambiguity of the features that makes the classification of some activities more difficult. Our approach using PART (Partial Decision Trees) has a low computational cost, few rules and high accuracy. This enables the classifier to be embedded on device (e.g.: Smartphone) and all processing to occur inside it.

Koster et al. [18] have focus on a system architecture for recommendation using context and activity recognition on health context. Our work can collaborate with one new approach for this system, but in the context of digital education.

4   Experimental Methodology

The output of each sensor is a time series of values representing a physical measurement. These values have a sequential order in time in which, each of them have a correlation with its closest neighbors. The linear acceleration sensor is an example of this kind of series in which the output $S = \{x_0, x_1, \cdots x_n\}$ is the set of x values between $0 \leq t \leq n$ interval [19].

For recognizing the user activities, we must represent S by a set of features. The more discriminant the features are, the easier it will be for the classifier to recognize and separate the activities. The flexibility of this approach allows us to use a different set of attributes for each sensor type. The features selected for the deployment of this work are: the average (AVG) linear acceleration module (acc), the average gyroscope module ($gyro$), the average pitch ($pitch$), the average roll ($roll$) and the standard deviation of the gyroscope module. Finally, the feature vector is:

$$[\|acc_{x,y,z}\|, \|gyro_{x,y,z}\|, \overline{pitch}, \overline{roll}, std(\|gyro_{x,y,z}\|)] \leftrightarrow \text{User Activity}.$$

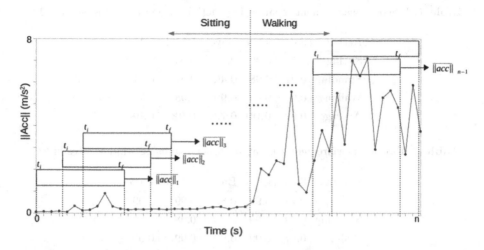

Fig. 3. Getting the feature's vector that represents the linear acceleration sensor by applying the sliding window approach.

We separate each sensor signals into frames with regular intervals of time using a sliding window approach (Fig. 3). After that, each frame is represented by its corresponding vector. The features values were obtained by applying the following equations:

$$\overline{\|acc_{x,y,z}\|} = AVG\left(\sqrt{acc_x^2 + acc_y^2}, acc_z^2\right), \tag{1}$$

$$\overline{\|gyro_{x,y,z}\|} = AVG\left(\sqrt{gyro_x^2 + gyro_y^2}, gyro_z^2\right), \tag{2}$$

$$\overline{pitch} = AVG(pitch), \tag{3}$$

$$\overline{roll} = AVG(roll), \tag{4}$$

$$std(\|gyro_{x,y,z}\|) = \sqrt{AVG(\|gyro_{x,y,z}\|^2) - M(\|gyro_{x,y,z}\|)^2}, \tag{5}$$

in which x, y and z vary according to the initial time (t_i) and the final time (t_f) of the frame. The pre-processing of the dataset and the feature extraction were carried out in MATLAB software. The classification step was performed using WEKA [20].

5   Experimental Results

The major challenge of our approach is to find the classification technique that maximizes the relationship between classification accuracy and computational complexity, enabling us to run the classifier in restricted hardware such as a smartphone. For this, we made comparisons between the classifiers described in Sect. 2, evaluating the F-Score and the accuracy with the equations:

Table 1. F-Score measurement separated by activity using a window sizes of 1 s.

Activity	SVM	kNN	Bayes	PART	C4.5
Sitting	0.77	0.99	0.81	0.99	0.99
Standing	0.21	0.98	0.46	0.97	0.97
Walking	0.90	0.98	0.90	0.98	0.98
Average	0.62	**0.99**	0.72	**0.98**	**0.98**

Table 2. F-Score measurement separated by activity using window sizes of 2 s.

Activity	SVM	kNN	Bayes	PART	C4.5
Sitting	0.78	0.99	0.88	0.99	0.99
Standing	0.29	0.99	0.64	0.98	0.98
Walking	0.91	0.99	0.90	0.99	0.99
Average	0.66	**0.99**	0.80	**0.99**	**0.99**

$$F - Score = \frac{2 \cdot precision \cdot recall}{precision + recall}, \tag{6}$$

$$Accuracy = \frac{TP + TN}{P + N}, \tag{7}$$

where TP, TN, P and N stands for: true positive, true negative, total of positives, and total of negatives, respectively. The F-Score quantify the balance between the total activity recognized among the total of activities that should be

STANDING   SITTING   WALKING

Fig. 4. Recognized activities

Table 3. Recognition accuracy by comparing different window sizes.

	SVM	kNN	Bayes	PART	C4.5
Frame with 1 s	73.57	99.02	78.22	98.57	98.63
Frame with 2 s	74.68	**99.58**	83.68	**99.15**	**99.08**

recognized properly. The Accuracy quantifies the closeness of the result achieved in relation to the optimal value [21].

Tables 1 and 2 shows the results of the F-score by activity, and Table 3 shows the Accuracy results for all activities tested. The experiments were repeated applying two different frame sizes and we count on the participation of 18 volunteers. The last line of Table 1 is the average of the three activities, highlighting in bold the best results. This metric shows a tie between the classifiers kNN, PART, and C4.5. We also note that the average values improve with the window size, mainly for SVM and Bayes. In Table 3, again, we observed an insignificant difference between the accuracy of kNN, PART, and C4.5.

From the results presented in this section, we may conclude that there is no significant difference in outcome between kNN, PART, and C4.5. However, kNN has a computational cost that grows proportionally to the dataset size ($O(n^2)$), where, in this case, we have 13591 instances. Meanwhile PART and C4.5 have a constant computational once the rules have been generated. Once trained, the classifiers SVM, Bayes, PART, and C4.5, have constant memory cost, whereas kNN needs to maintain a complete copy of the dataset in memory.

In the classification tree model generated by C4.5 each path between the root and the leaves might be considered a decision rule, but the procedure for generating rules is different from PART. The final C4.5 model in our experiment produced 96 leaves, different from PART that produced only 41 rules making this easier to program and embed on a smartphone. From testing the different window sizes, we observed that increasing the size improves the results because more points of the signals are used to calculate the mean and the variance. However, to avoid losing short term activities, we decided to not increase the size over two seconds.

6   Applications

In this work, we classify three activities: sitting, walking and standing (Fig. 4), therefore, two Android applications were built. One of them collects data from sensors for training and choice of the best algorithm of machine learning. The other app implements the algorithm chosen, i.e., the decision rules based on PART (described at Subsect. 2.2).

6.1   Application "Sensors" for Data Collect

The first app was implemented to collect data from the Linear Acceleration, Gyroscope and Orientation sensors, according to the flowchart of Fig. 5.

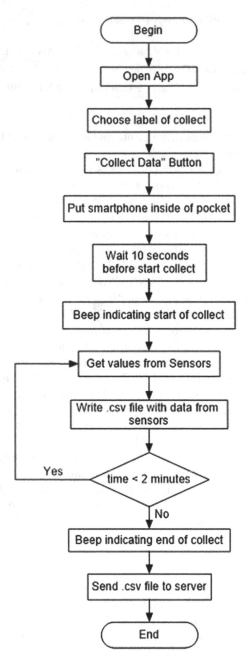

Fig. 5. Flowchart of Application for data collect from sensors

This application collects the labeled data of the three activities during two minutes. On the screen, the user can choose the activity for which they will gather information. Three steps are necessary to accomplish all the gathering for each

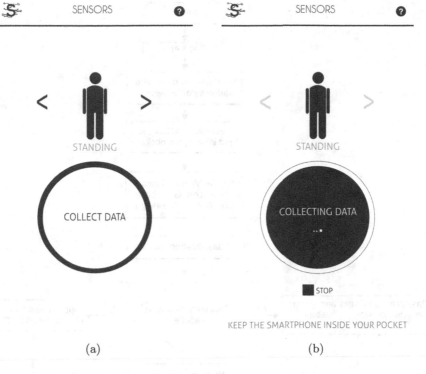

(a)   (b)

Fig. 6. Application Sensors: starting of collecting data.

Fig. 7. Application Sensors: ending of collecting data.

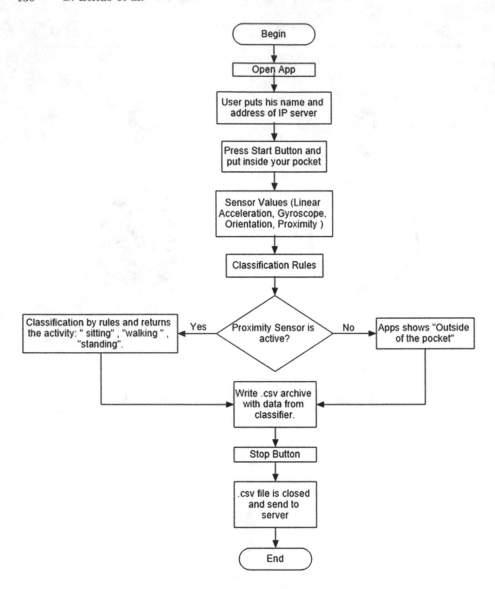

Fig. 8. Flowchart of Application for *Activity Recognition*

one of the activities: "Collect Data" (Fig. 6(a)), "Collecting Data" (Fig. 6(b)) and "Collected Data" (Fig. 7). After the gathering, the data is automatically sent to our server (connected to the internet).

6.2   Application of *Activity Recognition*

The second application was implemented using the 41 rules produced by PART as mentioned previously (Sect. 5) and works according to the flowchart of Fig. 8.

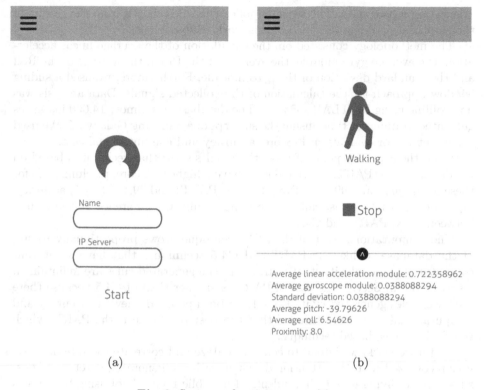

(a)   (b)

Fig. 9. Screens of activity recognition

Initially, the application only used the decision rules, using the values of Linear Acceleration, Gyroscope and Orientation sensors, but this failed if the device was not in the user's pocket while trying to classify some activity. Because of this, it was necessary to add information from Proximity sensor.

In Fig. 9, there are two screens. While the Fig. 9(a) shows the setup of Server's address, the Fig. 9(b) presents the details of the measures used for classification of activity and applying the decision rules of PART.

7   Conclusions

This paper detailed the methodology and experimental evaluation of the main supervised machine learning techniques to be adopted for the human activities recognition in technology education context. Data was collected from smartphone sensors because we consider that the vast majority of students already have them. For the experiments, we consider the recognition of the following activities: walking, standing and sitting.

We implemented two applications: the first collects data from various sensors (Subsect. 6.1), but for this experiment, we only use the gyroscope and accelerometer data, and the pitch and roll, which are calculated by software using the orientation sensor data. The second applies the rules chosen from the results of the empirical research described in this work (Subsect. 6.2).

The methodology consisted ofn the calculation of the average linear acceleration, the average gyro module, the average of the Pitch, the average of the Roll and the standard deviation of the gyro module. Furthermore, we used a sliding window approach for the calculation of the collected signals. Data analysis was done offline using MATLAB software. The database has almost 14,000 instances generated at different times using the smartphone Samsung Galaxy S5. We used three metrics for evaluation: F-Score, accuracy and computational cost.

From the accuracy point of view, the results show that techniques based on the decision tree (PART, C4.5) and kNN have a higher F-Score, reaching 99 % for these techniques; and 99.6 % (kNN), 99.1 % (PART) and 99.1 % (C4.5) accuracy. We conclude that, statistically, there is no significant difference at the results between kNN, PART and C4.5.

The computational cost of the kNN technique grows proportionally to size of the database, unlike the PART and C4.5 techniques that have a constant computational complexity if, after training, the generated rules are maintained. As we wrote in Sect. 5, the cost of PART is smaller than of C4.5 because there are fewer rules generated by it. Then, from both points of view i.e. accuracy and computational cost, we concluded that the best technique is the PART, which is a decision tree-based technique.

As future work, we intend to collect, analyze and correlate the rate of activities recognized with the attention deficit in order to generate inferences of possible signs of hyperactivity in students of a public high school using Samsung's Digital Education Platform.

Acknowledgements. The results presented in this paper were obtained through the project entitled *"Systems for Behavior Assessment and Intelligent Recommendation for Educational Environments and e-Health"* sponsored by *Samsung Eletrônica da Amazônia Ltda* under Brazilian Federal Law No. 8248/91; and FAPEAM through projects 1135/2011 (PRONEX) and 582/2014 (PROTI-PESQUISA).

References

1. Pentland, A.: Honest Signals. How They Shape Our World. MIT Press, Cambridge (2010)
2. Android Developers. http://developer.android.com/guide/topics/sensors/sensors_motion.html
3. Su, X., Tong, H., Ji, P.: Activity recognition with smartphone sensors. Tsinghua Science and Technology **19**(3), 235–249 (2014)
4. Kotsiants, S.: Supervised machine learning: a review of classification tecniques. In: Emerging Artificial Intelligence in Computing Engineering, pp. 3–24 (2007)
5. Kaghyan, S., Hakob, S.: Activity recognition using k-Nearest neighbor algorithm on smartphone with tri-axial accelerometer. Int. J. Inform. Models Analyses (IJIMA), Bulgaria **1**, 146–156 (2012)
6. Mitchell, T.: Machine Learning. McGraw-Hill Education, New York (1997)

7. Segaram, T.: Programming Intelligence Collective: Building Smart Web 2.0 Applications. O'Reilly Media, Sebastopol (2007)
8. Vapnik, V.: The Nature of Statistical Learning Theory. Springer, New York (1995)
9. Holsheimer, M., Siebes, A.P.: Data Mining: The Search for Knowledge in Databases. Technical report, Amsterdam (1994)
10. Hssina, B., Merbouha, A., Ezzikouri, H., Erritali, M.: A comparative study of decision tree ID3 and C4.5. Int. J. Adv. Comput. Sci. Appl. 4(2), 13–19 (2014)
11. Quinlan, J.R.: Induction of decision trees. Mach. Learn. 1, 81–106 (1986). Boston
12. Quinlan, J.R.: C4.5 Programs for Machine Learning, p. 7. Morgan Kaufmann Publishers, San Mateo (1993)
13. Frank, E., Witten, I.: Generating accurate rule sets without global optimization. In: Proceedings of the Fifteenth International Conference on Machine Learning, pp. 144–151. Morgan Kaufmann Publishers Inc., San Francisco (1998)
14. Zhang, S., McCullagh, P., Nugent, C., Zheng, H.: Activity monitoring using a smart phones accelerometer with hierarchical classification. In: Sixth International Conference on Intelligent Environments, pp. 158–163. IEEE (2010)
15. Khan, A.M., Lee, Y.-K., Kim, T.-S.: Accelerometer signal-based human activity recognition using augmented. In: IEEE Engineering in Medicine and Biology Society, pp. 5172–5175. IEEE (2008)
16. Tapia, E.M., Intille, S.S., Haskell, W., Larson, K., Wright, J., King, A., Friedman, R.: Real-time recognition of physical activities and their intensities using wireless accelerometers and a heart rate monitor. In: IEEE International Symposium on Wearable Computers, Boston (2007)
17. Long, X., Yin, B., Aarts, R.M.: Single-accelerometer-based daily physical activity classification. In: IEEE Engineering in Medicine and Biology Society, pp. 6107–6110. IEEE (2009)
18. Koster, A., Koch, F., Kim, Y.B.: Serendipitous recommendation based on big context. In: Bazzan, A.L.C., Pichara, K. (eds.) IBERAMIA 2014. LNCS, vol. 8864, pp. 319–330. Springer, Heidelberg (2014)
19. Khan, A., Muhammad, H., Seok-Won, L.: Exploratory data analysis of acceleration signals to select light-weight and accurate features for real-time activity recognition on smartphones. Sensors 13(10), 13099–13122 (2013)
20. Hall, M., Frank, E., Holmes, G., Pfahringer, B., Reutemann, P., Witten, I.: The WEKA data mining software: an update. SIGKDD Explor. Newsl. 11, 10–18 (2009)
21. Kansiz, A., Oguz, M., Guvensan, A., Turkmen, H.: Selection of time-domain features for fall detection based on supervised learning. In: World Congress on Engineering and Computer Science, San Francisco, CA, USA, pp. 23–25 (2013)

Author Index

Printed in the United States
By Bookmasters